VIRGINIA WOOLF

DATE DUE

JOHN LEHMANN

VIRGINIA WOOLF

with 136 illustrations

THAMES AND HUDSON

Frontispiece: Virginia Woolf at
52 Tavistock Square, in 1939.

First published in paperback in the
United States of America in 1999 by
Thames and Hudson Inc., 500 Fifth
Avenue, New York, New York 10110

Library of Congress Catalog Card
Number 98-61521
ISBN 0-500-26026-5

Printed and bound in Spain

In the volume of his autobiography called *Beginning Again*, Leonard Woolf wrote: 'Bloomsbury was and is currently used as a term – usually of abuse – applied to a largely imaginary group of persons with largely imaginary objects and characteristics.' He then went on to say, with what one can only describe as characteristically Woolfian self-contradiction: 'I was a member of this group, and I was also one of a small number of persons who did eventually form a kind of group of friends living in or around that district of London legitimately called Bloomsbury.'

The nucleus of this group of friends had been formed at Cambridge, at the turn of the century. Most of them were undergraduates at Trinity or King's College. All were outstanding intellectually, and many of them belonged to the secret Cambridge intellectual society, which had already existed for several generations, called 'The Apostles'. They shared, or came to share, certain attitudes to life, to thought and to artistic creation largely derived from their near-contemporary and friend, the philosopher G. E. Moore. His *Principia Ethica* influenced all of them, not only while they were at Cambridge, but in fact for the remainder of their lives.

The philosopher G. E. Moore, who influenced the circle of friends at Cambridge later called the Bloomsbury group

Several of these friends were to become famous in later years, notably Lytton Strachey as iconoclastic biographer of *Eminent Victorians* and *Queen Victoria*; Clive Bell as eminent art critic and (with Roger Fry, who only became closely associated with the group in 1910) impresario of the Post-Impressionist painters of the 'School of Paris' in England; J.M. (Maynard) Keynes (later Lord Keynes) as revolutionary economist of world-wide renown; and Leonard Woolf, who is remembered now, perhaps unfairly, rather as devoted husband of a famous wife than as editor, publisher and left-wing political theorist and educator. He was the son of an eminent Jewish Q.C., one of eleven children who were left in straitened circumstances when their father died in 1892.

Maynard Keynes from a photograph by Vanessa Bell

Bertrand Russell in a portrait by
Roger Fry

Desmond MacCarthy, the finest
dramatic critic of his generation, in a
portrait head by Quentin Bell

E. M. (Morgan) Forster; portrait by
Dora Carrington

Three other Cambridge men, all a little older, whose names have
always been connected with Bloomsbury, were Bertrand Russell, the
philosopher, held by most of them to be the most brilliant intellectually
of all; Desmond MacCarthy (like Russell, also an 'Apostle'), who
has been justly described as the finest dramatic critic of his generation;
and, seeming to appear and disappear like a mole in their midst,
E. M. (Morgan) Forster, the novelist. Duncan Grant, who in the eyes
of the public was to become the quintessential Bloomsbury artist,
was in fact a later arrival, only introduced by his cousin Lytton
Strachey in 1907.

There was one other friend in the original circle, like Clive Bell
never an 'Apostle' and outstanding rather for his looks and character
than for his mind: Thoby Stephen, the elder son of Sir Leslie Stephen,
distinguished Victorian man of letters and first editor of *The Dictionary
of National Biography*. He had, in his freshman year at Trinity, joined
the Midnight Society, a small reading club just founded, of which
Clive Bell, Lytton Strachey and Leonard Woolf were the leading
lights. Thoby had two sisters, Vanessa and Virginia, who became
intimately involved with Thoby's brilliant friends when their
University careers were finished. In 1907 Vanessa married Clive Bell,
on the rebound from the early death of Thoby which had occurred in
the late autumn of the previous year. And in 1912 Virginia, already
thirty years old, married Leonard Woolf, who had thrown up his
career in the Colonial Service (in Ceylon) in the hope of making
her his wife. Quentin Bell, younger son of Clive and Vanessa, in his
biography of his aunt has called it 'the wisest decision of her life'.

Virginia had a difficult childhood, which was nevertheless not without its advantages for a girl who seems almost to have been born with the intention of becoming a writer.

Leslie Stephen's first wife was Thackeray's daughter Harriet Marian (Minny). She died in 1875, leaving a daughter, Laura, who turned out to be mentally deficient and spent most of her life in institutions. Minny's sister Anne, known as Aunt Anny, was a novelist and a formidable presence in the Stephen household. A few hours only before Minny's death, the family was visited by Mrs Herbert Duckworth, a close friend of the Thackeray sisters and herself a widow with children. Her maiden name was Julia Jackson, and her mother Maria was one of seven famous Pattle sisters who had made their mark in mid-Victorian London society – artistic rather than intellectual. Mrs Cameron, the famous early photographer, was one of Julia's aunts; another, Sarah, as Mrs Thoby Prinsep was the slightly eccentric hostess of Little Holland House where the Pre-Raphaelite painters were frequent visitors. Julia very soon became confidante and consoler to Leslie, who in 1878 found that he was in love with her and married her. Within the next five years four children were born: Vanessa in 1879, Thoby in 1880, Virginia in 1882 and Adrian in 1883.

(*Above*) Sir Leslie Stephen, father of Virginia Stephen, a distinguished man of letters and first editor of *The Dictionary of National Biography*; an engraving after the painting by G. F. Watts

(*Above left*) Julia Duckworth (née Jackson) became Sir Leslie Stephen's second wife in 1878 and Virginia was their third child. This portrait photograph is by her aunt, Julia Margaret Cameron, the famous Victorian photographer.

22 Hyde Park Gate in 1975, but unchanged since the Stephen family lived there

The house at 22 Hyde Park Gate in which Virginia grew up was thus filled with children, and a great concourse of aunts and uncles and cousins were continually visiting. The family had some grand relations on Julia's side, but kept up few contacts with aristocratic society. It would seem that it was from Julia's ancestors, the Pattles, that Vanessa and Virginia inherited their outstanding good looks. The Stephens belonged in the main to the reasonably well-to-do upper-middle and professional classes, with the accent on intellectual achievement, and were connected with the famous evangelical Clapham Sect, which played such an important part in the abolition of slavery and the slave-trade. In his youth, Leslie had been ordained in order to take up his Fellowship at Trinity Hall but, like many other earnest and thoughtful Victorians, lost his faith a few years later. He left Cambridge, became a journalist, and championed the cause of the North during the American Civil War; with the result that among his many friends in the world of literature were a number of distinguished Americans, including Oliver Wendell Holmes and Henry James, while the poet James Russell Lowell, for some years American Ambassador at the Court of St James's, became Virginia's godfather.

Virginia grew up in a literary atmosphere. Her father had a large library, and at first directed Virginia's voracious appetite for reading with careful choices; but by her middle teens he was sufficiently impressed by her intelligence and discrimination to allow her a free run of the library. This was, surely, an exceptional freedom for a girl in Victorian times, and of immense benefit to her in her formation as a writer. As far as English literature went, it would seem, then, that Virginia taught herself; but a little later she was given private lessons in Latin and Greek by Janet Case and Walter Pater's sister Clara. A liberal education for an intelligent girl at any time; but, as *A Room of One's Own* makes abundantly clear, Virginia never got over a feeling of resentment that she as a female had to learn in rather a restricted way at home, while her brother Thoby as a male was enjoying all the advantages of an expensive education at Cambridge.

The library at 22 Hyde Park Gate was, one can say with certainty, the chief formative influence for Virginia's developing mind; for her

Thoby Stephen, elder brother of Virginia Stephen

Vanessa Stephen, Stella Duckworth and Virginia Stephen, *c.* 1896

Talland House, St Ives: holiday home of the Stephen family at the turn of the century

imagination, one can say with almost equal certainty, the over-whelming experiences were her holidays in Cornwall. In the year of Virginia's birth, her father had bought Talland House, on the high ground above the bay at St Ives, and from that time until just before Julia's death the family migrated there annually in the late summer. The excitement among the children was immense, and the joys of boating, fishing, playing on the seashore, and watching the passing ships by day and the beams of the Godrevy Lighthouse at night, sank deep into their memories, and for Virginia were transmuted into the symbols of her art, emerging not only, though most famously, in *To the Lighthouse* but also in *Jacob's Room* and *The Waves*. 'Oh, how beautiful!' Mrs Ramsay exclaims in *To the Lighthouse*. 'For the great plateful of blue water was before her; the hoary Lighthouse, distant, austere, in the midst; and on the right, as far as the eye could see, fading and falling, in soft low pleats, the green sand dunes with the wild flowing grasses on them, which always seemed to be running away into some moon country, uninhabited of men.' And what could be more perfectly expressive of the unspoilt wonder of childhood than the passage where Nancy wades to 'her own rocks' and searches 'her own pools' on the shore:

She crouched low down and touched the smooth rubber-like sea anemones, who were stuck like lumps of jelly to the side of the rock. Brooding, she changed the pool into the sea, and made the minnows into sharks and whales, and cast vast clouds over this tiny world by holding her hand against the sun, and so brought darkness and desolation, like God himself, to millions of ignorant and innocent creatures, and then took her hand away and let the sun stream down. Out on the pale criss-crossed sand, high-stepping, fringed, gauntletted, stalked some fantastic leviathan (she was still enlarging the pool), and slipped into the vast fissures of the mountain side. . . .

In St Ives there were not only the wonders of the sea but also the pleasures of cricket, in which Virginia to the surprise of all distin-guished herself as a 'demon bowler', and nocturnal expeditions to

Virginia and her sister Vanessa playing cricket, St Ives, 1894

trap moths, of which she wrote so vividly many years later in her long essay 'Reading'.

As often happens in literary households where the children are impatient to emulate their elders, Virginia and Thoby started a little hand-written periodical between them, the *Hyde Park Gate News*, which appeared or was intended to appear weekly. Virginia was only nine when the first number was concocted and, as Thoby was at school most of the time, one can fairly safely attribute the writing almost entirely to Virginia. Only a few numbers have survived, but it seems to have come to a definite end in April 1895. One particularly interesting (and comically naïve) feature of the early numbers is the inclusion of a serial by Virginia, 'A Cockney's Farming Experience', and 'The Experiences of a Paterfamilias', her first known attempt at a 'novel' – there could hardly have been anything before.

It is tempting, again, to see the seed of a famous novel in an entry in the *Hyde Park Gate News* for 12 September 1892:

On Saturday morning Master Hilary Hunt and Master Basil Smith came up to Talland House and asked Master Thoby and Miss Virginia Stephen to accompany them to the light-house as Freeman the boatman said that there was a perfect wind and tide for going there. Master Adrian Stephen was much disappointed at not being allowed to go.

The Godrevy lighthouse at St Ives: a central image in *To the Lighthouse*

Virginia Stephen as a girl in her early teens with her father, Sir Leslie

The first great crisis in the lives of the Stephen children was the death of their mother, Julia, in 1895. Virginia, at thirteen, was deeply attached to her and was aware of the bond of happy love that had existed between her and her husband. The effect on Sir Leslie was catastrophic. Worn already by his literary labours, and above all by his work on the *Dictionary*, he had come to depend immoderately on his wife's support to look after the household, the children and all the details of the social life they lived. He became querulous, self-pitying to a grotesque degree, and inordinately demanding on his children. The chief victim at first was Julia's daughter by her first marriage, Stella Duckworth, who with great courage unquestioningly accepted the burden of carrying on in Julia's place.

Virginia, already ravaged by grief at her mother's death, which she described as 'the greatest disaster that could happen', and dismayed by the tensions of the new situation, had her first breakdown. It seems that she remembered very little of her mental state, but recalled a racing pulse with a feeling of great excitement she could not control, followed by a state of the deepest depression and self-accusation. She wrote nothing, though she still read feverishly in spite of the fact that her lessons had been stopped and her doctor prescribed long hours of outdoor exercise.

She recovered; but was almost immediately faced with a new situation, created by Stella's engagement to Jack Hills, her marriage and departure on honeymoon to Italy, and Sir Leslie's gloomy struggle to adapt himself to the change. Though radiantly happy in her marriage, Stella's sense of duty had obliged her to give way to Sir Leslie's ill-concealed distress to the extent of agreeing to live at the house across the street. Unfortunately, she came back from her honeymoon seriously ill, partially recovered, but a few months later died in the course of an operation. It was July 1897, only a little more than two years after Julia's death.

Stella's death exacerbated the difficulties of home life at Hyde Park Gate. During the next seven years Sir Leslie's gloom and self-pitying tantrums increased. They were wreaked in the main on Vanessa, who as eldest surviving daughter had to take Stella's place. Every week, when Vanessa presented the household bills, Sir Leslie would utter prolonged groans, and wail that ruin faced them all. The ever-recurring scene was ridiculous (and entirely unjustified by the facts), but appalling for Vanessa, whose heart gradually hardened against her father. Virginia still loved him, but found it increasingly difficult not to be outraged by his grossly selfish and inconsiderate behaviour towards her beloved sister. The division in her emotions cannot have been propitious for a highly strung girl who had already had one serious breakdown. The result was that when Sir Leslie finally died of cancer in 1904 she had a far more alarming breakdown, which one cannot call anything but madness. As always afterwards, it started slowly, with headaches and fits of bewildered irritation; then the deeper nightmare developed, in which she passed through manic tortures of self-accusation and guilt about her father; she was attended by three nurses who became incarnations of evil in her mind; frantically, she resisted all attempts to feed her, and when she was taken down to the country she attempted to commit suicide by throwing herself out of a window. As the crisis slowly passed, she lay in bed imagining that the birds outside her window were singing in Greek, and (according to her nephew Quentin Bell) that King Edward VII was concealed among the bushes, uttering streams of the filthiest possible language.

During this breakdown she was greatly helped by the devoted care of an older woman friend, Violet Dickinson, with whom she had obviously fallen in love. Violet was a friend of the Duckworths, tall, not particularly good-looking or talented, but a strong and balanced personality, high-spirited, warm-hearted, with an outstanding gift for selfless sympathy and understanding. This was not the first time that Virginia had fallen in love with a person of her own sex. A few years earlier, her heart had been totally captured by a cousin, Madge Vaughan, the daughter of John Addington Symonds. Madge was attractive and had a romantic aura about her; she had been brought up among the Swiss Alps, was intensely interested in the arts and was

Virginia Stephen in 1903

a writer herself. Virginia may well have had Madge in mind when creating the character of Sally Seton in *Mrs Dalloway*.

Virginia's passions for Madge Vaughan and Violet Dickinson cannot have been anything but 'pure'. In fact Virginia showed every sign of being sexually retarded. It has been suggested that this was due to emotional traumas caused by her half-brother, George Duckworth, who, Virginia alleged, began to make a habit of fondling her in an extremely intimate if not grossly indecent way when she was still an adolescent. She also claimed that the other half-brother, Gerald, indulged in such attentions when she was even younger. Perhaps the full truth will never be known about this; but it is certain that George, who eventually married Lady Margaret Herbert, behaved in later years as a model friend and affectionate brother.

Many years after her father's death, Virginia wrote in her diary: 'His life would have entirely ended mine. What would have happened? No writing, no books; – inconceivable.'

The Bedroom, Gordon Square, by
Vanessa Bell, 1912

Lytton Strachey at work; pastel by
his brother-in-law Simon Bussy

The Stephen children had long decided that, as soon as they could, they would leave Hyde Park Gate, that house of unhappy memories beset by the raven-like flocks of family mourners. Now that they were free, they chose a large, roomy house well away from Kensington, just north of the British Museum, No. 46 Gordon Square. The houses that had been built on the Duke of Bedford's estate in Bloomsbury, at the beginning of the nineteenth century, had a certain elegance and charm if little distinction; but the relations were appalled. It was *not* a good address, and they could not understand what had come over the children. This in itself was a recommendation to Vanessa, Virginia and their two brothers; they would not only be making a fresh start, they would also be escaping from the ever-watchful and critical eyes of uncles, aunts and elder cousins.

Thoby, who had now come down from Cambridge and was reading for the Bar, decided to make a meeting-place for his Cambridge friends in the new house, on Thursday evenings. There they could pursue the enthralling discussions begun at Trinity, without any deference to the London social world and its strict conventions, and be joined by his two intelligent sisters, Vanessa and Virginia. This was the real beginning of Bloomsbury, though Leonard Woolf is, I think, right in maintaining that it did not become self-consciously a group, or circle, until some years later.

Saxon Sydney-Turner; painting by
Vanessa Bell, 1908

Clive Bell at Virginia Stephen's
cottage at Studland, Dorset, 1910

The chief visitors at those Thursday evening gatherings were:
Lytton Strachey, whose erudition, cutting wit and malicious sense of
humour made him an object of fear as well as fascination to those who
were not among his intimates; Clive Bell who, though he belonged
by upbringing to the county world of hunting and shooting, was well
able to hold his own in intellectual discussions among the Moore-ites,
and was already deeply interested in the latest developments in painting
across the Channel, an aspect of his personality that his friends were
not at that time fully aware of; Desmond MacCarthy, who half-
belonged to that 'other' world of London 'society', where he shone as
a brilliant talker as well as a man of immense charm and kindly wit;
and Saxon Sydney-Turner, that enigmatic mute of Bloomsbury,
much lauded by his friends, who was always going to produce a great
book or a great musical composition, but never in fact did anything
at all. The two Stephen sisters, it seems, remained very silent on
Thursday evenings, and may well have been shocked at first by the
novelty of the frankness with which their brother's friends discussed
everything under the sun, including sex and its deviations. Leonard
Woolf was the only one of the original circle who did not attend these
ceremonies, as he had just embarked for Ceylon as an administrator
in the Colonial Service; but he has left a shrewdly observant description of the impression the sisters made on him when he first met them

in Cambridge during a visit to their brother Thoby. 'Vanessa and Virginia', he writes in *Sowing*,

were also very silent and to any superficial observer they might have seemed demure. Anyone who has ridden many different kinds of horses knows the horse who, when you go up to him for the first time, has superficially the most quiet and demure appearance, but, if after bitter experience you are accustomed to take something more than a superficial glance at a strange mount, you observe at the back of the eye of this quiet beast a look which warns you to be very, very careful. So too the observant observer would have noticed at the back of the two Miss Stephens' eyes a look which would have warned him to be cautious, a look which belied the demureness, a look of great intelligence, hypercritical, sarcastic, satirical.

Their new independence had also released in the Stephen children a great desire for foreign travel. Virginia had already visited Italy and Spain since her father's death, and in 1906 a great expedition to Greece, long dreamed of, was organized. Thoby and Adrian set off ahead, and Virginia, Vanessa and Violet Dickinson followed soon after, reuniting with the brothers at Olympia in the middle of September. For a group of English people educated in ancient Greek literature and civilization, the adventure was endlessly exciting; but it resulted in disaster. Vanessa, Violet and Thoby were probably incautious in drinking unboiled milk in the country places they visited; in any case, Vanessa was already unwell by the time the three

Clive Bell on the balcony of 46 Gordon Square

18

of them arrived in Patras and, after struggling on as far as Constantinople, she returned to England with Virginia in attendance. Thoby had gone ahead, but when they reached London he was already ill with a high temperature. Violet was also badly infected, and Thoby's serious condition had to be concealed from her. She and Vanessa recovered; but Thoby, perhaps because the doctors wrongly diagnosed malaria, died in late November from the typhoid fever he had in fact contracted.

Thoby's death was a shattering blow, from which, it seems, Virginia never entirely recovered, though it did not cause the kind of mental crisis that had followed the deaths of her mother and father. Years later, when she had finished writing *The Waves*, in which Percival is to a great extent modelled on Thoby, she planned at first to dedicate the novel to his memory.

The most important immediate result of Thoby's death for Virginia was Vanessa's decision to marry Clive Bell only two days later. This meant that Virginia and her younger brother Adrian would have to find another home, as it was quite clear that they would be *de trop* in the new household at No. 46. They eventually took a house at 29 Fitzroy Square, not too far to make intercourse with Gordon Square difficult, but far enough to assure independence.

Virginia Stephen; a charcoal drawing by Francis Dodd, 1908

Vanessa Bell at Charleston, *c.* 1920

Vanessa Bell painting; by Duncan Grant, 1913

Vanessa Bell; a bust by M. Gimond, c. 1922–6

Vanessa, now deeply absorbed in her ambition to become a painter as well as in her marriage, seemed rather to close doors on an exclusive set of intimates than wish to continue the old free and easy weekly gatherings. Virginia and Adrian soon decided to continue them on their own, in Fitzroy Square. Their *salon*, if one can call it by such an elegant name, showed itself to have rather a different accent in the next few years. In addition to the old stalwarts of the inner Cambridge circle, they invited not only a number of other friends of that circle, such as Sydney Waterlow, Henry Lamb, Charles Tennyson, Edward Hilton Young, but also women friends who could scarcely be called intellectuals, such as Lady Beatrice Thynne and Lady Godolphin Osborne, as well as Margaret Vaughan and Janet Case. And then, a year or two later, came the important addition of Lady Ottoline Morrell, that eccentric escapee from the aristocratic world, with her deep and thrilling voice, her almost Habsburg chin and bizarre dress, who gave the impression of towering benignly but formidably above the social scene. One night she brought along Augustus and Dorelia John and very soon after swept all of them into her own more worldly *salon* in Bedford Square, where they met an entirely different set which included Winston Churchill, Raymond Asquith and Lord Henry Bentinck.

The Virginia of these Fitzroy Square years was very different from the silent and perhaps rather scandalized girl of Thoby's early soirées. She had gained self-confidence, she could talk as frankly about sex as anyone, and she could make devastating comments about other people's opinions and tastes that often wounded rather more than they were intended to, because fundamentally she liked people, liked lively and friendly conversation full of jokes, and was intensely curious about the lives of the people she met. Nevertheless, all her life she had a sharp tongue, and a sharp pen, too – which often showed in her letters and her diary. A trait that was to become deeply characteristic now first showed itself: she would seize on some salient aspect

Adrian and Virginia Stephen on the lawn of 'The Steps', Playden; painting by Vanessa Bell, *c.* 1908

Virginia Woolf in her mother's dress, photographed by Marianne Beck, 1927

of a person she had just been introduced to, and immediately begin to build a superstructure of fantasy on it, more or less inventing that person's life for him or her. She would also do this with unknown people she saw sitting across from her in a train compartment, or encountered on a shopping expedition. A striking example of this in her writings is the concluding passage of the sketch *An Unwritten Novel*:

And yet the last look of them – he stepping from the kerb and she following him round the edge of the big building brims me with wonder – floods me anew. Mysterious figures. Mother and son. Where are you? Why do you walk down the street? Where tonight will you sleep, and then, tomorrow? . . . Wherever I go, mysterious figures, I see you, turning the corner, mothers and sons; yes, you, you, you. I hasten, I follow. This, I fancy, must be the sea. Grey is the landscape, dim as ashes; the water murmurs and moves. If I fall on my knees, if I go through the ritual, the ancient antics, it's you, unknown figures, you I adore: if I open my arms, it's you I embrace, you I draw to me – adorable world!

Quentin Bell coined an admirably appropriate phrase when he wrote that Virginia's imagination 'was furnished with an accelerator but no brakes'.

Vanessa Bell; painting by Duncan
Grant, c. 1918

The two Stephen sisters, as their circle of acquaintances widened,
were very soon famous for their beauty. Leonard Woolf has written
of them:

Vanessa was, I think, usually more beautiful than Virginia. The form of her features
was more perfect, her eyes bigger and better, her complexion more glowing. If
Rupert [Brooke] was a goddess's Adonis, Vanessa in her thirties had something

of the physical splendour which Adonis must have seen when the goddess suddenly stood before him. To many people she appeared frightening and formidable, for she was blended of three goddesses with slightly more of Athene and Artemis in her and her face than Aphrodite. . . . Virginia was a very different kind of person beneath the strong family resemblances in the two sisters. When she was well, unworried, happy, amused and excited, her face lit up with an intense almost ethereal beauty. She was also extremely beautiful when, unexcited and unworried, she sat reading or thinking. But the expression, even the shape of her face, changed with extraordinary rapidity as the winds of mental strain, illness or worry passed over its surface. It was still beautiful, but her anxiety and pain made the beauty itself painful.

Rosamond Lehmann, who came to know Virginia in the middle 1920s, gives a more acute description of her actual physical appearance:

She was extremely beautiful, with an austere intellectual beauty of bone and outline, with large melancholy eyes under carved lids, and the nose and lips, the long narrow cheeks of a Gothic madonna. Her voice, light, musical, with a throaty note in it, was one of her great charms. She was tall and thin, and her hands were exquisite. She used to spread them out to the fire, and they were so transparent one fancied one saw the long fragile bones through the live skin.

David Garnett has written that, as she spoke, 'excitement would suddenly come as she visualized what she was saying, and her voice would crack like a schoolboy's, on a higher note. And in that cracked high note one felt all her humour and delight in life.'

Just before she moved with Adrian to Fitzroy Square, Virginia had embarked on her serious career as a professional writer. She began to write reviews for the *Guardian*, and also for *The Times Literary Supplement*, encouraged on the latter by that remarkable and perceptive editor Bruce Richmond, thus starting a connection that lasted all through her life. She also wrote longer articles for the monthly *Cornhill* magazine. She took immense trouble about all these pieces, often rewriting half a dozen times. To back them up, she had the immense, insatiable reading of her girlhood, but in reviewing a particular book she would often reread all the relevant previous material with the most conscientious care. She loved her work, and her style and authority developed as appreciative editors demanded ever more of her. At the same time she began her first novel, originally called *Melymbrosia* but eventually *The Voyage Out*, which took her at least six years to write, and was rewritten from beginning to end half a dozen times. Unusually, for in her later life she never showed her work to anyone until at least the first draft was finished, she turned to Clive Bell for advice in the course of her work, and found in him an acutely intelligent critic.

It was inevitable, of course, that such a beautiful and talented girl should have her suitors, in spite of the rather forbidding, bluestocking

Virginia Stephen and Clive Bell at Studland Bay, Dorset, *c.* 1910

Lytton Strachey and Clive Bell criticizing works of art; a drawing by Henry Lamb

aspect she presented to the world. She had a flirtation with Walter Headlam, poet and Hellenist and almost old enough to be her father, which was cut short by his death in 1908. In 1909, Edward Hilton Young appears to have proposed to her, but, in spite of much that might have recommended him, was rejected, as was Sydney Waterlow a year later. She also had a long flirtation with the philandering Clive, which upset Vanessa but came to nothing in spite of Clive's importunities. There was probably no one in her whole life whom Virginia loved more than her sister, and one cannot help suspecting that there was a slight element of revenge in this flirtation. Vanessa's marriage had taken her away from Virginia; obscurely, Virginia was getting her own back.

But in 1909 a tragi-comic episode took place, which was more painful for Virginia than the absurdity of the circumstances might suggest. Lytton Strachey proposed to her, and was immediately accepted. Directly afterwards, he realized he could not go through with

it, and that it would be no solution at all to the complicated problems of his personal life. He envisaged the possibility that she might want to kiss him, and was appalled. He confessed his second thoughts to Virginia in another meeting, and showing great tact and affectionate understanding, she released him. And yet, though she knew all about his homosexual tendencies and male *amours*, there is little doubt that she would have liked him as a husband. She had known him so long, she wanted to be married to a man whose intellect she could respect, and lacking sexual passion herself, she was probably not disturbed by the possibility that the union might never be consummated – unlike those women who marry homosexuals in the conviction that they can convert them.

Curiously enough, it was Lytton himself who, with prescient insight only shortly before, had suggested in a letter to Leonard Woolf in Ceylon that he, Leonard, ought to marry her. Leonard replied: 'Do you think Virginia would have me? Wire to me if she accepts. I'll take the next boat home.' Two years later he did in fact come home on a year's leave, and began his suit to Virginia almost at once.

A famous and extraordinary episode took place at this time: the hoax played upon H.M.S. *Dreadnought*, the newest and greatest warship in the Royal Navy. The hoax had been devised by Virginia's brother Adrian and his Cambridge friend Horace Cole, already well known for his practical jokes. The idea was to hoodwink the Navy into thinking that they were to receive a visit from the Emperor of Abyssinia and his entourage. Astonishingly, the ludicrous deception was successful. On 10 February 1910 the Emperor, impersonated by Anthony Buxton, and his suite which included Duncan Grant and Virginia (who was roped in at the last moment), all with heavily blackened faces, and Horace Cole himself as a bogus Foreign Office official in charge, were received with ceremony on board the great warship. They were shown round, all the secrets of the ship were revealed to them, and Adrian as interpreter relied on mispronounced

(*Opposite*) The Dreadnought hoax. Front page of *The Daily Mirror*, 16 February 1910. Virginia Stephen is first from the left and Duncan Grant is the Abyssinian Prince on the extreme right

The Daily Mirror

THE MORNING JOURNAL WITH THE SECOND LARGEST NET SALE

No. 1968.   Registered at the G.P.O. as a Newspaper.   WEDNESDAY, FEBRUARY 16, 1910   One Halfpenny.

HOW THE OFFICERS OF H.M.S. DREADNOUGHT WERE HOAXED: PHOTOGRAPH OF THE "ABYSSINIAN PRINCES" WHO HAVE MADE ALL ENGLAND LAUGH.

All England is laughing at the practical joke played a few days ago on the officers of H.M.S. Dreadnought by five men and a young woman, who, with the aid of elaborate "make-ups," passed themselves off as Abyssinian princes, an interpreter, and a representative of the Foreign Office, and were accorded royal honours and shown all over the mighty battleship by Admiral Sir William May and the Dreadnought officers. Above is a photograph taken in London just before the party started for Weymouth on their visit to the Dreadnought. (A) The young woman of the party who disguised herself as "Prince Sanganya." (B) "Prince Mandok." (C) "Herr George Kauffmann, the German interpreter." (D) "Prince Makalen, the chief of the Abyssinian princes." (E) "Prince Mikael Golen." (F) "Mr. Herbert Cholmondely, the Foreign Office attaché." The lady and the man who posed as "Herr Kauffmann" are brother and sister.

quotations from Virgil in explaining to the pseudo-Abyssinians what the officers were telling them. The cream of the joke to Adrian was that the Flag-Commander on board the *Dreadnought* was their own cousin William Fisher. All might have been well, but Horace Cole felt that their triumph would be incomplete without the Press being told how they had scored off the august authorities of the Admiralty. A furious row developed, and in the end honour was rather absurdly saved by the abduction of Duncan Grant by a young naval party and his token corporal punishment. Virginia seems to have enjoyed herself very much; but it was the last as well as the first occasion in which she indulged in such public practical joking. It may, however, have been due to the excitement of this episode that Virginia's health later the same year approached a danger-point and obliged her to undertake a rest-cure.

A year later, the lease of 29 Fitzroy Square came to an end. Virginia and Adrian took the lease of a four-storeyed house in Brunswick Square (No. 38), and divided it up among themselves and their friends. Maynard Keynes and Duncan Grant, whose lover he had become, shared the ground floor, Adrian had the second and Virginia

Duncan Grant; pencil drawing by Henry Lamb, 1911. Grant and Lamb were members of the Friday Club and the Camden Town Group at the time of this drawing

Duncan Grant, Maynard Keynes and Clive Bell at Charleston

Adrian Stephen and his wife Karin (née Costelloe) at about the time of their marriage, *c.* 1914

the third; Leonard was now offered a bedroom and sitting-room on the fourth floor. Early in 1912 Virginia also took a five-year lease on Asheham House, in a hollow of the Sussex Downs near the Lewes–Seaford road, and Leonard, who had helped her to find the house, was a frequent visitor there. The result was, of course, that they were seeing a great deal of one another both in town and in the country. As the year wore on, Leonard found himself more and more deeply in love. Virginia at first adopted evasive tactics, but in the spring he felt himself sufficiently encouraged to take the decisive step of resigning from the Colonial Service, in which he had distinguished himself and in which the highest prizes were within his grasp. Finally, at the end of May, he and Virginia became engaged. In his account of the occasion, in *Beginning Again*, Leonard wrote:

I had lunch with Virginia in her room and we sat talking afterwards, when suddenly Virginia told me that she loved me and would marry me. It was a wonderful summer afternoon and we felt that we must get away from London for a time. We took the train to Maidenhead and I hired a boat and rowed up the river to Marlow and then we came back and dined at the riverside restaurant in Maidenhead. We both felt that in those ten hours from after lunch to midnight when we got back to Brunswick Square we had seemed to drift through a beautiful, vivid dream.

They were married on 10 August 1912.

Asheham House; painting by
Vanessa Bell, 1912

'Asheham as you perceive is
surrounded by sunshine. . . .' Sketch
by Dora Carrington in a letter to
Lytton Strachey dated 29 January
1917

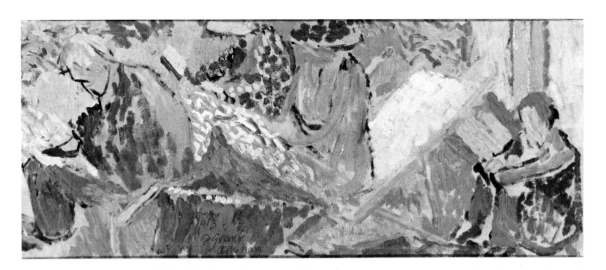

Asheham Group (Henri Doucet, Virginia Woolf, Vanessa Bell and Adrian Stephen); painting by Duncan Grant, 1913

Leonard Woolf and Virginia at Asheham House

Leonard Woolf at work; painting by
Vanessa Bell

The Woolfs took a peripatetic honeymoon through the Continent,
France, Spain and Italy. On this honeymoon Leonard evidently
discovered what must have been for him, a normal man with a
passionate nature, a painful disappointment: Virginia, though she
loved him, did not like sexual intercourse, and could not respond to
him as he had hoped and had a right to expect. Worse was to come.

On their return Virginia went back to her work on the final draft of
The Voyage Out, revising it with a feverish intensity. In March 1913
it was submitted to the family firm of Duckworth, and accepted with
enthusiasm. It was not, however, published until 1915, because once
more Virginia was gradually going mad. Anyone who has followed
Virginia Woolf's history with care, or was present during any of the
great mental crises of her life, will know that in her adult years these
attacks or threats of returning madness almost always came in the last
stages of the composition of one of her novels. They occurred in a

lesser degree when she was finishing *The Waves* in 1931, and (more alarmingly) *The Years* in 1936; and finally in the last stages of writing *Between the Acts* in 1941, when she chose to commit suicide rather than endure the nightmare again. The attack, which became acute in the summer of 1913, lasted until the autumn of 1915, with a period of comparative lucidity and balance between February 1914 and February 1915. It was not only the worst yet, but the most serious in the whole of her life. In September 1913 she and Leonard had returned from the country for a brief visit to Brunswick Square. While Leonard was out, she took an overdose of veronal. When he returned he found her unconscious, and with immense presence of mind got Geoffrey Keynes, Maynard's younger brother and a house surgeon at St Bartholomew's Hospital, who was lodging on the top floor, to drive him at top speed through the traffic to obtain a stomach-pump. At 6 a.m. the next morning Virginia began to recover.

It appears likely, though astonishing, that Leonard did not know when he married her how serious Virginia's mental instability was. 'The goat's mad, of course' was probably the way her family referred to her former crises (her family nickname was 'Goat' or 'Billy Goat', for some lost reason). That she suffered from a deep, almost certainly congenital, manic-depressive condition, beyond the understanding

Virginia Woolf; pencil and
watercolour sketch by Vanessa Bell

Ka (Katherine) Cox, who looked
after Virginia Woolf during her
breakdown in 1913; painting by
Duncan Grant, 1912

of most doctors of the time, and outside the range of psychoanalytical treatment, was something he had to learn the hard way.

During her illness, Virginia owed a great deal to the devoted ministrations of Katherine Cox, known as 'Ka', who came into her life about 1911 in the company of Marjorie Strachey, one of Lytton's many sisters, and her friends from Newnham College in Cambridge. Ka Cox was one of a younger Cambridge group, revolving round Rupert Brooke, who came to be known in Bloomsbury as the 'Neo-Pagans'. Their relations with Bloomsbury were friendly without being intimate; they were anti-religious, certainly brilliant, but equally certainly, in spite of such episodes as nude bathing parties (in one of which Virginia joined), more conventional in their attitudes towards sex. When Virginia made her suicide attempt, Ka was in the house and was sufficiently alarmed to telephone Leonard to hurry home. Afterwards she went with her to Dalingridge, George Duckworth's large and well-staffed house in Sussex, which he had generously offered them. In this crisis, Ka played the role that Violet Dickinson had played in 1904; and undoubtedly each in her turn helped to save Virginia's life.

Virginia's illness on this occasion was a repetition, but on a far more horrifying scale, of what she went through in 1904. One cannot doubt that Leonard was right in saying that his wife's breakdowns were not simply more acute examples of other people's nervous collapses, but that in the course of them she definitely passed from a state of sanity to a state of insanity, in which her awareness of and adjustment to the outside world were totally obliterated. He gives a truly appalling description of her manic phase during the 1913–15 breakdown, in which she passed from the depressive state of refusing to eat and being overwhelmingly oppressed by feelings of guilt and despair, to a state of the wildest over-excitement, violent with her nurses (she had four) who (as before) had been turned into malevolent fiends in her mind, and talking incessantly for several days, at first partially coherently, and then totally incoherently, 'a mere jumble of dissociated words'. After which she fell into a coma; from which she emerged utterly exhausted, but on the very slow road to recovery.

What is peculiarly astonishing about these fits of madness is that afterwards Virginia not only could remember much of what she had gone through, but was even able to use the experiences objectively in her writing; as in the portrait of Septimus Warren-Smith in *Mrs Dalloway*. It seems to me to point to some almost unfathomable strength in Virginia's spiritual make-up. Quentin Bell has described how her friends and relations believed that, after this shattering experience, her mind and character would be permanently affected. Nevertheless, the first thing she did, when normality returned to her, was to take up work on her second novel, *Night and Day*, which is not

Virginia Woolf Seated; painting by
Vanessa Bell, 1912

only sane but almost boringly so. And for the whole decade of the
1920s, during which she produced or prepared her masterpieces and a
continuous stream of acutely intelligent, perceptive and witty literary
criticism, she had no serious relapses, though she was in poor health
during the later months of 1925 and had a briefly anxious period when
she was finishing *To the Lighthouse* the following year. This may have
been partially due to the strict régime of total quiet and rest which
Leonard insisted on the moment he detected the first signs of a return
of her disorder, but it certainly does not point to anything like a
curtailment of mental powers or transformation for the worse of her
character; in fact the reverse.

During one of the lucid intervals in her illness, early in 1915, Virginia
and Leonard, searching for a new London abode, discovered, fell in
love with, and eventually acquired the lease of a beautiful eighteenth-
century house in Paradise Road, Richmond: Hogarth House. For a

time after their marriage they had taken rooms in Clifford's Inn, though returning to Brunswick Square from time to time. Now they moved finally out of both.

The war was already in its second year; but apart from the restrictions of liberty and the rationing which the whole population of Britain had to endure, Bloomsbury did not suffer in any particularly painful way. To say that may appear to be rather callous about the deaths of friends and relations, of Rupert Brooke, for instance, and Leonard's brother Cecil, in the course of the war; but Leonard himself, not a pacifist, was excused military service because of a congenital muscular tremor, which would certainly have made him extremely dangerous, rather to his own fellow soldiers than to the enemy, with a rifle in his hands. Lytton Strachey was also finally excused, on the ground of extreme physical debility. Maynard Keynes was working in the Treasury; and most of the rest, declaring pacifist principles, agreed to do agricultural work, either in Sussex or on Lady Ottoline Morrell's farm at Garsington in Oxfordshire. They included a new recruit, the future novelist David Garnett, then in his early twenties, son of the famous Edward Garnett who as publisher's reader had recommended *The Voyage Out* to Duckworth. There were, of course, the air raids and Zeppelin raids; but they were in no way as destructive or frightening as in the 1939 War.

Rupert Brooke; woodcut by Gwen Raverat, 1919

Lady Ottoline Morrell; drawing by Henry Lamb, *c.* 1912

The Pond at Garsington, a painting by Mark Gertler, 1916

37

Virginia Woolf and Lytton Strachey at Garsington, in a photograph taken by Lady Ottoline Morrell

(*Below left*) Lytton Strachey, Clive Bell and Duncan Grant at Eleanor House, Sussex, the home of St John and Mary Hutchinson, close friends of the Bells and the Woolfs, 1915

(*Below right*) Duncan Grant and E. M. Forster standing behind Clive Bell and Mary Hutchinson, in the Charleston Farm garden

(*Opposite above*) Charleston Farm, near Lewes, first taken by Clive and Vanessa Bell in 1916 and thereafter their country home, another meeting-place for the Bloomsbury group while Leonard and Virginia Woolf lived in the nearby village of Rodmell

(*Opposite below*) Duncan Grant's studio at Charleston, *c.* 1930–31

Farringdon Street, Holborn Viaduct, in 1925, near where Leonard and Virginia Woolf bought their first hand-press to start the Hogarth Press

When the Woolfs had settled into Hogarth House and Virginia was on the way to recovery, both of them agreed that it would be therapeutic for Virginia and in general a very pleasant occupation if they were to start printing on their own. One day in March 1917, they were walking along Farringdon Street towards Holborn Viaduct, when they happened to pass a small printing supply firm with all the paraphernalia of printing displayed in the window. Excited by this discovery, they went in to make inquiries and found to their surprise and delight that the man in charge of the shop was not only prepared to sell them a small hand-press and all the necessary implements and material to start printing, including some Old Face type, but assured them that if they read a sixteen-page pamphlet he pressed on them, they would find printing child's play. The whole outfit cost them just under £20. When it was delivered to them at Hogarth House, they immediately set it up in the dining-room and started to teach themselves to print. A month later, they had learned enough to be able to print a page of a book or a pamphlet. Virginia did most of the setting (often with some of the type upside-down) and then Leonard, having corrected her mistakes, would lock up the type in the chase and set about the machining. Their first effort was a thirty-two-page booklet consisting of two stories, one by each of them. They bought some gaily patterned paper for the binding, and stitched it themselves. They sent out a circular to friends and others they thought might be interested, and printed about 150 copies, charging 1s. 6d. each. So began the Hogarth Press, which was to become a source of great pleasure to them in the early years (as well as an important factor in Virginia's recovery), to acquire considerable fame, make them money, but in the end turn into an anxious, time-consuming burden. And yet, right to the end of Virginia's life, the Press had one supreme advantage: she never had to bow to the possible editorial carping of professional publishers, nor fit her plans for work

THE HOGARTH PRESS

Telephone   Hogarth House
Richmond 496   Paradise Road
                                    Richmond
                                     Surrey

LIST OF PUBLICATIONS.

NEW PUBLICATIONS.

Stories from the Old Testament. Retold by
    LOGAN PEARSALL SMITH, author of
    Trivia.   4s. 6d. net.
Paris, a Poem. By HOPE MIRRLEES, author
    of *Madeleine*.   3s. net.

TO BE PUBLISHED SHORTLY.

The Story of the Siren. By E. M. FORSTER.
    2s. 6d. net.

PREVIOUS PUBLICATIONS.

VIRGINIA WOOLF
    The Mark on the Wall. Second edition.
    1s. 6d. net.
    Kew Gardens. With woodcuts by
    VANESSA BELL. Second edition. 2s. net.
KATHERINE MANSFIELD
    Prelude.   3s. 6d. net.
T. S. ELIOT
    Poems. 2s. 6d. net.   *Out of print.*
J. MIDDLETON MURRY
    The Critic in Judgment.   2s. 6d. net.
LEONARD & VIRGINIA WOOLF
    Two Stories.   *Out of print.*

Advertisement included at the back of the Hogarth Press edition of Gorky's *Reminiscences of Tolstoi*, 1920

T. S. Eliot, in a drawing by
Wyndham Lewis, 1938

Katherine Mansfield

to their needs and invitations. Eight years later she was to write in
her diary:

How my handwriting goes downhill! Another sacrifice to the Hogarth Press, yet
what I owe the Hogarth Press is barely paid by the whole of my handwriting.
Haven't I just written to Herbert Fisher refusing to do a book for the Home University
series on Post-Victorian? – knowing that I can write a book, a better book, a book
off my own bat, for the Press if I wish! To think of being battened down in the hold
of those University dons fairly makes my blood run cold. Yes, I'm the only woman
in England free to write what I like.

During the next three years, the new amateur Hogarth Press added
four important books to its tiny list. Luck, or far-sighted acumen?
Probably a bit of both, but probably also another factor: that Bloomsbury by that time represented an *avant-garde* intellectual attitude that
was naturally congenial to new writers who felt they were making a
break with the past. Leonard and Virginia had come to know
Katherine Mansfield (with whom Virginia's relations were always
extremely ambivalent), her husband John Middleton Murry, the
American-born poet T. S. Eliot who had settled in London, and an
eccentric and extremely intelligent Russian Jew, S. S. Koteliansky,
known as 'Kot', who had become a friend of D. H. Lawrence and
the Murrys, and was almost certainly introduced to the Woolfs by the
latter.

In 1918 they published Katherine Mansfield's *Prelude*, one of her
most famous short stories, but though they set up the type themselves,
Leonard did the machining on the press of a friendly local printer. The
next year they printed and bound the first edition of Virginia's short
story *Kew Gardens*, but an enthusiastic review in *The Times Literary
Supplement* sold this edition out very fast, and they had to go to
another friendly printer for a second edition of five hundred copies.
The same year (1919) they printed a small volume of seven new
poems by T. S. Eliot, whose first poems *Prufrock* had been published
by the Egoist Press in 1917. Four years later Eliot gave them *The Waste
Land*, the original edition of which they printed and bound themselves;
now one of the rarest and most sought-after books in modern English
literature. Meanwhile, in 1921, Virginia had decided to publish
Monday or Tuesday, which contained not only *Kew Gardens* but seven
more of her new experimental pieces with woodcuts by Vanessa: it
was set up by Leonard and Virginia, but printed badly, on atrocious
paper, by one of their friendly printers. The year before, they had
published Gorky's *Reminiscences of Tolstoi*, in a translation in which
Koteliansky and Leonard collaborated. This was reprinted almost
at once, by a commercial printer, and went on being reprinted for
many years.

All these books were extremely small, and had nothing to recom-
mend them in the way of fine printing or production; but the contents,

The cover of Virginia Woolf's *Kew Gardens*, designed by Vanessa Bell, 1919

it is scarcely an exaggeration to describe as revolutionary, and their success, though it would no doubt have appeared negligible to an established publisher, encouraged Leonard and Virginia to continue on their way to turn what had started as a hobby into a regular publishing business. Even to the very end of Virginia's life they continued to set up and machine an occasional small book on their own press, but the bulk of their publications were handled by big commercial printers and binders. None of their own work was ever done in their country homes, but at Hogarth House in Richmond, or 52 Tavistock Square, to which they were to move in 1924.

Virginia Woolf's first two novels, *The Voyage Out* (1915) and *Night and Day* (1919), follow a roughly conventional pattern. That is, each has a story which moves in time from the beginning of the book to the end, characters who are described both in outward appearance and inward thought and feeling by the narrator, and a plot in which they act on one another and develop until a final conclusion or resolution is reached.

The Voyage Out is by far the more interesting of the two, in spite of certain obvious faults of structure and characterization. It appears to set out as a social comedy, in the manner of E. M. Forster perhaps, but as it goes on it acquires, intermittently, a new dimension, a visionary and poetic quality that foreshadows the novels of Virginia Woolf's maturity. This first novel has several strikingly unusual features. Most extraordinary, perhaps, is that it ends with the apparently causeless and meaningless death of the young, virginal heroine, Rachel Vinrace, whom we first meet when she is about to embark on a voyage to South America on one of her father's ships, and that this death occurs just after she has discovered the supreme happiness of love. Unique, too, in Virginia's fiction, is the fact that the setting is entirely imaginary, for Virginia had never been on such a voyage nor in any part of South America, though she had made a trip from Liverpool to Oporto in the spring of 1905. When the party, which includes her aunt and uncle, arrive at their destination, they find staying in the same seaboard town a number of English people, in particular two young men who are close friends: Terence Hewet, a would-be novelist, and St John Hirst, ugly, intellectually arrogant, no social charmer but with a sincere passion for truth. He is, in fact, rather a Bloomsbury character, and might have sat at the feet of G. E. Moore. Terence and Rachel begin to feel an attraction for one another, but both have a strong resistance to being too closely involved emotionally with another human being: Terence because he wants to go on writing his novel, Rachel because she loves her inviolate existence, her solitude and her music. This is a situation that Virginia never explores again in her later novels. An especially interesting under-current is the relationship between Rachel and her aunt, Helen, who appears at first to be selflessly devoted to her niece. As the story progresses, however, one senses that this devotion has a strong element of jealous possession. There is a scene, at the point where Rachel and Terence discover at last that they love one another, in which Helen appears to fall on Rachel and wrestle with her on the ground. It reads like an hallucination, but one cannot be sure. We only know that Virginia rewrote the passage again and again, slightly changing its implication in each version.

Scattered throughout the book are first hints, intimations of themes that become more dominant in the later novels: the sense of the beauty of the natural scene, of *things* and the elements, when no human beings are there (as one finds it for instance in the 'Time Passes' sequence in *To*

Arnold Bennett; drawing by B. Partridge, *c.* 1926

the Lighthouse); the awareness of the deep, prehistoric past (as one finds it, for instance, in *Between the Acts*); the strangeness of a ship full of passengers and activity which turns into nothing but a blurred point as it fades away over the horizon, and the corresponding strangeness of life actually going on busily on land when it has all but vanished to the watchers on a ship (which forms an essential poetic element in the final section of *To the Lighthouse*); and the deep concern with marriage, its value and meaning in life (a theme so strongly developed in all the later novels after *Jacob's Room*).

The Voyage Out leaves one with the sense of many questions about human life and society posed, but tantalizingly answered only, if at all, in riddles and moments of intense poetic suggestion, especially in the penultimate scenes. Not so *Night and Day*, which Leonard Woolf once described as one of the two 'dead' novels Virginia wrote, that is without, or almost without, the visionary quality that was to become her hallmark. The other one, in his view, was *The Years*, and it is significant that each of these was written after, and as a kind of mental relaxation from a major visionary achievement, in the case of *The Years* from *The Waves*. *Night and Day* is a leisurely, readable, almost old-fashioned novel, from which it would be impossible to deduce that the author had recently come out of an appalling bout of madness, or – as Katherine Mansfield observed – that the shattering earthquake shock to the sensibility of a generation, the Great War, had just occurred. Full of sensitive feeling and acute social observation, it has scarcely any of the poetic overtones of *The Voyage Out*, though a beauty of language that enchants by itself; and one brilliantly realized character, the heroine's mother Mrs Hilbery. The tower of fiction, the edifice of all the established conventions of the novel, stands four-square; but already Virginia was beginning to feel a deep dissatisfaction, and before *Night and Day* was completed she was experimenting with some short sketches which, like firebrands tossed in at a window, were soon to send the whole edifice up in a blaze. The first, 'The Mark on the Wall', had already appeared in *Two Stories*. They were published in a small collection, *Monday or Tuesday*, in 1921.

H.G. Wells

During the years immediately following her recovery in 1915, Virginia's output, not only in fiction, but also in reviews and essays, most of them in *The Times Literary Supplement*, the *Athenaeum* and the *New Statesman*, was remarkably prolific. One of them, 'Modern Fiction', written in the spring of 1919, is extremely important, not only for its attack on the outstanding novelists of the day, but also as a kind of manifesto of what she now wanted to write herself. Are the works of these novelists (Wells, Bennett and Galsworthy), she asks, a true reflection of life as we experience it? Her answer is against them. 'If we tried to formulate our meaning in one word,' she writes, we should say that these three writers are materialists. It is because they are concerned not with the spirit but with the body that they have disappointed us, and left us with the feeling that the sooner English fiction turns its back upon them, as politely as may be, and marches, if only into the desert, the better for its soul . . . whether we call it life or spirit, truth or reality, this, the essential thing, has moved off, or on, and refuses to be contained any longer in such ill-fitting vestments as we provide.

From this condemnation, Virginia Woolf moves on to her famous manifesto or blueprint for the new novelist:

Look within, and life, it seems, is very far from being 'like this'. Examine for a moment an ordinary mind on an ordinary day. The mind receives a myriad impressions – trivial, fantastic, evanescent, or engraved with the sharpness of steel. From all sides they come, an incessant shower of innumerable atoms; and as they fall, as they shape themselves into the life of Monday or Tuesday, the accent falls differently from of old; the moment of importance came not here but there; so that, if a writer were a free man and not a slave, if he could write what he chose, not what he must, if he could base his work upon his own feeling and not upon convention, there would be no plot, no comedy, no tragedy, no love interest or catastrophe in the accepted style, and perhaps not a single button sewn on as the Bond Street tailors would have it. Life is not a series of gig-lamps symmetrically arranged; life is a luminous halo, a semi-transparent envelope surrounding us from the beginning of consciousness to the end. Is it not the task of the novelist to convey this varying, this unknown and uncircumscribed spirit, whatever aberration or complexity it may convey, with as little mixture of the alien and external as possible?

It is interesting to note that from her general denunciation she excepts Thomas Hardy, Joseph Conrad, James Joyce, whose *Ulysses* was at that time appearing in the *Little Review* (though she was later to have a revulsion against what seemed to her the obscenity of the completed work), and, above all, the Russians because of their essential concern with 'the soul and heart'.

In 1915 she had begun to write a fairly regular diary, and kept it, with brief intervals, until her death in 1941. After the war her husband published a volume of extracts from it, telling us that he had mainly chosen those passages in which she revealed her own thoughts about her writing, how she planned each book, her changes of mood in the process of creation, and the state of hypersensitivity to criticism which would build up in her when the first printed copies were sent out to friends and to reviewers. *A Writer's Diary* is only a fragment of the whole work, which was an acclaimed literary event when it was eventually published. As it is, the extracts make an utterly absorbing book, essential for the understanding of her creative processes, and an overwhelmingly impressive record of a life devoted single-mindedly to authorship. On 26 January 1920, more than a year before *Monday or Tuesday* was published, she writes in it, having that afternoon arrived 'at some idea of a new form for a new novel':

Original drawing for the jacket of *A Writer's Diary*, by Vanessa Bell; it contained Leonard Woolf's extracts from Virginia Woolf's diary between 1919 and her death, and was published in 1953

Suppose one thing should open out of another – as in an unwritten novel – only not for 10 pages but 200 or so – doesn't that give the looseness and lightness I want; doesn't that get closer and yet keep form and speed, and enclose everything, every‐ thing? My doubt is how far it will enclose the human heart – Am I sufficiently mistress of my dialogue to net it there? For I figure that the approach will be entirely different this time: no scaffolding; scarcely a brick to be seen; all crepuscular, but the heart, the passion, humour, as bright as fire in the mist. . . . I suppose the danger is the damned egotistical self; which ruins Joyce and Richardson to my mind: is one pliant and rich enough to provide a wall for the book from oneself without its becoming, as in Joyce and Richardson, narrowing and restricting?

The phrase 'stream of consciousness' (originally invented by William James) has been used to describe the technique Virginia Woolf was now to begin to employ for her fiction. It had already been experimented with – as she implies – by Dorothy Richardson in *Pointed Roofs* and by James Joyce in *Ulysses*, the incomplete manuscript of which Harriet Weaver had shown to the Woolfs in 1918. Much discussion has gone on as to who influenced whom, but it seems to me that one can say little more than that the idea of using such a technique was clearly 'in the air', part of the new consciousness which the most sensitive post-war novelists and poets were struggling to express; and though all three, James Joyce, Dorothy Richardson and Virginia Woolf, developed a style in which 'stream of consciousness' played its part, each used it in a different way. As the sequence of 'Miriam' novels which followed *Pointed Roofs* showed, Dorothy Richardson never properly solved the problems of selection and structure which a 'stream of consciousness' technique poses. In the short sketches of *Monday or Tuesday*, Virginia did attempt something which would follow the darting of the mind from one train of thought to another; but even in these sketches there is less inconsequence than might appear at first reading. As she had suggested in 'Modern Fiction', her basic aim in the novels she now envisaged was to capture a different reality from what Wells, Bennett and Galsworthy assumed to be reality, something that would express the 'semi-transparent envelope' of consciousness in all its complexity, the soul with its intuitions of the eternal as in the greatest poetry, rather than the material world. And to achieve this aim she saw that she needed to jettison 'plot' in the accepted sense, and achieve an aesthetically satisfying structure by other means. Most of the other conventional props of the novel, in which the author-narrator (however concealed) moves his characters with careful scene-shifting from one place to another, from one moment of time to the next moment chosen, also had to go – 'no scaffolding, scarcely a brick to be seen'. Lightness, speed, the use of symbols in imagery, were of the essence of such an attempt. In *Jacob's Room* (1922) she made her first full-length experiment.

In the summer of 1919, just before Peace was signed, Leonard and Virginia found a new country home in the little village of Rodmell, a few miles from Lewes in Sussex. The deeds of Monk's House went back to 1707; it had been inhabited by many families during the course of two hundred years, but, as Leonard only discovered in the last years of his life, never by any monks. In *Beginning Again* he writes:

We had often noticed the house and garden before 1919, for walking up or down the lane between Rodmell church and the village street you could look over the wall into the orchard and garden and catch a glimpse of the back of the house. The orchard was lovely and the garden was the kind I like, much sub-divided into a kind of patchwork quilt of trees, shrubs, flowers, vegetables, fruit, roses and crocus tending to merge into cabbages and currant bushes.

Monk's House, Rodmell, seen from the road

They moved into Monk's House in September, and it became their permanent country home. A great deal of Virginia's writing was done there, *Jacob's Room* the first novel.

The first thing one notices about *Jacob's Room* is the radical change that has taken place in Virginia Woolf's technique since her first two novels. There is, in fact, very little use of 'stream of consciousness' as yet; but though there is still a story, of the most skeletal kind, there is no plot; and all the conventional transitions from one place or time to another have been abolished. Changing from one character to another, from one episode to another, the author wastes no time at all. She works by a series of impressionistic flashes, the light of her narrative moving with astonishing speed and suddenness from one point of fragmented thought or observation to another, to build up her total impression, whether in dialogue or description.

I have said there is no plot; in fact, one begins to wonder, as one reads on, whether the action, such as it is, is of basic importance. The highlights of *Jacob's Room* are not moments of revelation about character, or moments of drama in the development of character, but moments of poetic vision. On Cambridge, for instance, she writes in a famous passage:

They say the sky is the same everywhere. Travellers, the shipwrecked, exiles, and the dying draw comfort from the thought, and no doubt if you are of a mystical tendency, consolation, and even explanation, showers down from the unbroken surface. But above Cambridge – anyhow above the roof of King's College Chapel – there is a difference. Out at sea a great city will cast a brightness into the night. Is it fanciful to suppose the sky, washed into the crevices of King's College Chapel, lighter, thinner, more sparkling than the sky elsewhere? Does Cambridge burn not only into the night, but into the day?

It is not without intention that the book ends with reverberations and echoes, and Bonamy's cry of 'Jacob! Jacob!' in the empty room, which picks up the same cry on the seashore at the very beginning, suggesting so poignantly transience, loss and anguish.

Virginia Woolf took two years, from 1922 to 1924, to write her next novel, *Mrs Dalloway*, though it was evidently in her mind for some time before she began to put it down. In it she shows far greater mastery of her new technique. The problem of structure is effectively solved by having the action confined to one place, London, and one day – the day of Clarissa Dalloway's party, in which the passing of time is marked by the booming of the hours by Big Ben. (The novel was originally to be called *The Hours*.) But whereas the impressionism of *Jacob's Room* had reduced her characters to glimpses, shadow impressions, in *Mrs Dalloway* her use of 'stream of consciousness' builds them up as real persons with astonishing skill. Each of the main characters – Clarissa Dalloway herself, her former lover back from India, Peter Walsh, the shell-shocked survivor from the war, Septimus Warren-Smith, and his pathetic Italian wife Lucrezia, and Clarissa's once-adored girlhood friend Sally Seton – is seen both inwardly in her or his own thoughts, and as reflected in the thoughts of the others; thoughts, memories, judgments, which range over the past as well as the present, so that by the end one has the impression that one knows them intimately, in the full significant history of their lives as well as in their outward appearance and quirks of behaviour (Peter Walsh's opening and shutting of his pocket-knife, for instance).

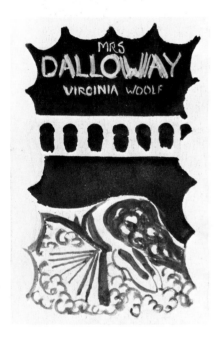

Drawing for the jacket of Virginia Woolf's *Mrs Dalloway*, by Vanessa Bell, 1925

The most daring and original aspect of the design, or tapestry of the book, is the weaving together of two entirely separate threads of narrative: Clarissa's party and the day-long preparation for it, and the madness and eventual suicide of Septimus Warren-Smith. Virginia was aware of the difficulty of the task she had set herself, and when she had finished it she was afraid that the reviewers would pounce on the apparent disjointedness as a serious flaw; and yet it was basic to her conception that the mad consciousness of Septimus should be placed as a foil against the worldly parade of Clarissa's party. At the end, the famous specialist, Sir William Bradshaw, who has attended Septimus, comes to the party and apologizes for being late as a result of Septimus's

The Wonderful Month of May; house-tops seen from Regent's Park where Peter Walsh had his dream in *Mrs Dalloway*; painting by Walter Sickert

suicide; but this is only a superficial link. The real link is between the characters of Clarissa and Septimus, so that, in a sense, one can almost talk of their being opposite sides of the same coin. Clarissa, now in her middle age, is aware that she has sacrificed something deep in her nature by becoming a worldly and successful political hostess – the something that made her fall in love with the reckless and dazzling Sally in her girlhood. Peter Walsh is skilfully used as another foil to show up what Clarissa has lost, what she has outwardly turned into. But, like Septimus, she is obsessed with the idea of death, as a solution to a life whose basic futility she glimpses in moments of intuition. The lines from the song in *Cymbeline*, 'Fear no more the heat o' the sun', run in her head. When she hears Sir William talking of Septimus's suicide at the party, she reflects:

A thing there was that mattered; a thing, wreathed about with chatter, defaced, obscured in her own life, let drop every day in corruption, lies, chatter. This he had preserved. Death was defiance. Death was an attempt to communicate, people feeling the impossibility of reaching the centre which, mystically, evades them; closeness drew apart; rapture faded; one was alone. There was an embrace in death. . . . There were the poets and thinkers. Suppose he had had that passion, and had gone to Sir William Bradshaw, a great doctor, yet to her obscurely evil, without sex or lust, extremely polite to women, but capable of some indescribable outrage – forcing your soul, that was it – if this young man had gone to him, and Sir William had impressed him, like that, with his power, might he not then have said (indeed she felt it now), Life is made intolerable; they make life intolerable, men like that?

At one moment in the book, and one only, Virginia abandons her technique and steps out as narrator-commentator; the passage is startling because it is so completely outside the fabric she is weaving. It is, in fact, a denunciation of Sir William and his kind; and one is aware of a passion behind it that must surely have arisen from Virginia's contempt for and horror of the specialists who failed utterly to understand her case in 1913:

Worshipping Proportion, Sir William not only prospered himself but made England prosper, secluded her lunatics, forbade childbirth, penalised despair, made it impossible for the unfit to propagate their views until they, too, shared his sense of proportion. . . . But Proportion has a sister, less smiling, more formidable, a Goddess even now engaged – in the heat and sands of India, the mud and swamp of Africa, the purlieus of London, wherever in short the climate or the devil tempts man to fall from the true belief which is his own – is even now engaged in dashing down shrines, smashing idols, and setting up in their place her own stern countenance. Conversion is her name and she feasts on the wills of the weakly, loving to impress, to impose, adoring her own features stamped on the face of the populace. . . .

Virginia Woolf; pencil and wash sketch by Wyndham Lewis, 1921

In fact, the lust for power, which Bradshaw reveals so sickeningly, is one of the main themes of the book; Lady Bruton is a hard and power-seeking hostess; Miss Kilman's devotion to Elizabeth is simply another form of the same lust.

Mrs Dalloway abounds in the most profound poetic images, often of great beauty, often of terror, which emerge with ease and naturalness from the rapid flow of the narrative; like fireworks breaking in shower after shower of different coloured stars as they fall. At one point she introduces a more extended, more complex image, one of the most mysterious and evocative in all her work: Peter Walsh's dream. He has fallen asleep in Regent's Park, at the other end of a bench where an elderly grey nurse is seated knitting, a baby in a perambulator beside her: 'In her grey dress, moving her hands indefatigably yet quietly, she seemed like the champion of the rights of sleepers, like one of those spectral presences which rise in twilight in woods made of sky and branches. The solitary traveller, haunter of lanes, disturber of

Bus traffic on the Strand in 1923, as Clarissa Dalloway might have seen it

ferns, and devastator of great hemlock plants, looking up suddenly, sees the giant figure at the end of the ride. . . .' So it goes on for several pages; in its elaboration and intensity, one cannot help feeling, it records some actual hallucinatory experience of Virginia herself.

All her life Virginia found certain scenes highly charged with emotion and poetry, and kept returning to them. One was the sea-shore; another, old houses which had been inhabited by many generations, or abandoned by a life which had once filled them; and the third, London. *Mrs Dalloway* was, among many other things, a celebration of London, the tremendous, colourful metropolitan stir and bustle, the romantic grandeur of Royalty and Imperial politics, the great parties of the social season, Big Ben striking the hours so solemnly, the noble peace of St Paul's, the laughing children and the squirrels in the leafy parks, the blaze of flowers in the shop windows, and the ceaseless animation of the traffic-laden streets. Parts of *Jacob's Room* were a sketch of this scene, always so stimulating to her; in other parts she went back to the seaside life of her childhood. Her next novel was to be fully concerned with that seaside life.

Clive Bell with Angelica, Stephen
Tomlin and Lytton Strachey at
Charleston, *c.* 1925

The Hogarth Press: front page of
the autumn 1924 catalogue, with a
drawing by Vanessa Bell

THE HOGARTH PRESS

52 TAVISTOCK SQUARE, LONDON, W.C.1.

AUTUMN ANNOUNCEMENTS

1924

Between the publication of *Jacob's Room* in October 1922 and that of *Mrs Dalloway* in May 1925, the Woolfs travelled and led an active social life in the midst of Virginia's steady literary output. Leonard Woolf accepted the literary editorship of the *Nation* in March 1923 (which he kept only for three years), and immediately after, before he started work, he and Virginia made an expedition to Spain and Paris. During 1923 and 1924 they spent several week-ends at Garsington with Lady Ottoline Morrell, where their fellow guests included, apart from old friends such as Lytton and Tom Eliot, a number of younger writers, Edward Sackville-West, Lord David Cecil, L. P. Hartley, and the composer Lord Berners. At Monk's House in the summer of 1923 again they had numerous week-end guests, among them Lytton and Morgan Forster, and younger lights of Bloomsbury, including Francis Birrell and Raymond Mortimer. In September 1923 they stayed at Lulworth with Maynard Keynes and the ballet-dancer Lydia Lopokova whom he was to marry in the following year. But the major event of 1924 was the discovery in January, by Virginia, of a new house in London: both of them had begun to feel the strain of making the journey from Richmond to the West End so frequently, though Leonard had doubts about the wisdom of bringing Virginia so close to the hurly-burly. She bought the lease early in July: No. 52 was on the south side of Tavistock Square, like 46 Gordon Square a typical Bloomsbury terrace-house. She and Leonard moved there from Richmond in March. The Hogarth Press with its offices and printing gear was established in the basement, while a studio at the back of the basement, built on what must have been a small London garden, became Virginia's writing-room, while at the same time being used as a stock-room for the Press. The Woolfs occupied the top two floors as living quarters, and allowed the sitting tenants, a firm of solicitors, Messrs Dollman and Pritchard, to occupy the ground and first floors. No. 52 Tavistock Square remained the Woolfs' London home until 1939.

Virginia Woolf at about the time when she completed *Mrs Dalloway*

After the publication of *Mrs Dalloway*, while she was working intensively on *To the Lighthouse* in the summer of 1925, Virginia had a serious collapse. It appears to have been more physical than mental, and in all likelihood due to the combination of continuous creative and critical work and too much social activity. Her low state of health continued all during the rest of that year and into the early months of 1926. When she was able to work properly again she found that *To the Lighthouse* began to flow from her pen with ease and rapidity. 'Never', she noted, 'have I written so easily, imagined so profusely.' Though this euphoria had, as usual, evaporated by the time she reached the last stages, the book was finished early in 1927.

In her continuous experimentation in new forms, new vessels to contain what she experienced as the essential reality of existence,

Virginia Woolf in the late 1920s

Virginia was never satisfied with any one solution, however effective it might seem. In *To the Lighthouse* she makes a further variation in the revolutionary design she had woven so tentatively in *Jacob's Room*, so daringly and with such assurance in *Mrs Dalloway*. Again, there is no plot, and only the slightest of stories round which to crystallize her total vision. Again she used the 'stream of consciousness' technique, or as I prefer to call it, internal impressionism (for it is never more than apparently random), to build up her characters; but the problem of time is solved in a new way. *To the Lighthouse* consists of three sections. In the first, all the action takes place on one afternoon and evening, while the Ramsay family are holidaying with their friends in the Hebrides (for Scotland read Cornwall); in the last, on one morning, many years later after the war, when the survivors gather again in the long-deserted holiday house. In between, there is a phantasmal acceleration of time, in which six or seven (or perhaps ten?) years pass in twenty-five pages, in which human happenings, marriage, childbirth, destruction and death in battle, occur only in passing reference or in brackets, so elemental is the scene, so dreamlike the pace. It is a vision of a world abandoned by human beings, who have left only the evocative debris of former living and feeling. Even Mrs McNab and Mrs Bast, charwomen who eventually arrive to make the house ready for the return of the family, seem more like creatures of myth than women of flesh and blood.

Round this simple framework, Virginia Woolf has created what is probably the most visionary and formally perfect of her novel-poems: a new kind of poem about the meaning and mystery of life and human relations, which explores the secret movements of the mind, and the role and power of the creative artist. The central theme is the married relationship of Mr and Mrs Ramsay. It is not to play the identification game to say that they are portraits of the Stephen parents, for Virginia herself admits it and believed that in writing the book she had laid their ghosts. Vanessa wrote to her about Mrs Ramsay: 'It is almost painful to have her so raised from the dead. You have made one feel the extraordinary beauty of her character, which must be the most difficult thing in the world to do.'

Mrs Ramsay dominates the book, even in the last section where she is only an insistent memory in the thoughts of Lily Briscoe. She is shown as unreflectingly bossy, with an itch for matchmaking, masterful and yet subtly submissive to her husband; continuously active, almost always engaged in some task for her children or household, some errand to the poor, but in her intervals of repose shedding a light of peace and intuitive understanding around her. She is a creator, with her own special gift, able to 'pour erect into the air a rain of energy, a column of spray, looking at the same time animated and alive as if all her energies were being fused into force, burning and

(*Opposite*) View from Virginia Woolf's study in Monk's House

illuminating', and her masterpiece is the *bœuf en daube* dinner-party, which becomes a symbol of the human mind achieving order and beauty against the forces of darkness and chaos. The picture is given an added touch of magic by Mr Ramsay beginning to recite the poem *Luriana, Lurilee* as they are about to leave the table, the lilting, chiming lines of which are interwoven with the remainder of the scene. Afterwards, Mrs Ramsay reflects: 'They would, she thought, going on again, however long they lived, come back to this night; this moon; this wind; this house; and to her too.'

Mrs Ramsay is also a mystic, as a poet is a mystic, feeling a communion between herself and the lighthouse; 'the long steady stroke, the last of the three', which she watches with fascination, 'as if it were stroking with its silver fingers some sealed vessel in her brain whose bursting would flood her with delight'; feeling also an empathy when alone with inanimate things, 'trees, streams, flowers; felt they expressed one; felt they became one; felt they knew one, in a sense were one.' She has moments of an incommunicable sense of deep spiritual calm and illumination, when 'all the being and the doing, expansive, glittering, vocal, evaporated; and one shrunk, with a sense of solemnity, to being oneself, a wedge-shaped core of darkness, something invisible to others. . . . This core of darkness could go anywhere, for no one saw it. They could not stop it, she thought, exultingly. There was freedom, there was peace, there was, most welcome of all, a summoning together, a resting on a platform of stability.'

By contrast, Mr Ramsay is entirely immersed in the world of the intellect, a philosopher with a 'splendid mind' but none of the creative or intuitive gifts of his wife. He is a monster of egotism, demanding as of right support and appreciation from all around him, though secretly haunted by a sense of failure; thought of as a tyrant by his children, but devotedly admired by charmless disciples like Charles Tansley. Virginia represents the working of his mind in a brilliant and often-quoted image: the alphabet image. 'He reached Q. Very few people in the whole of England ever reached Q. . . . But what after Q? What comes next? After Q there are a number of letters, the last of which is scarcely visible to mortal eyes, but glimmers red in the distance.' But Mr Ramsay cannot get beyond Q to R, though he summons all his powers to do so. She draws him with sympathetic perception, but also with a sly touch of humour. It is impossible not to smile as he pounds round the garden, glaring, and muttering to himself 'stormed at with shot and shell', or with heavy self-pity 'the father of eight has no choice'. It is equally impossible not to admire him as he sits absorbedly reading in the boat that takes them to the lighthouse at the end, while James suddenly discovers an affinity between his father and himself, and then leaps 'lightly, like a young man, holding his parcel, on to the rock'.

Virginia Woolf, Angelica Bell,
Leonard Woolf and Judith Bagenal
at Cassis, *c.* 1927–8, at the time of the
publication of *To the Lighthouse*

To the Lighthouse has probably been the favourite novel of the
majority of Virginia Woolf's readers. It has the same beauty of
language, the same speed and lightness of narration as *Mrs Dalloway*,
the same dazzling abundance of poetic imagery which profoundly
illuminates and never merely decorates. At the same time, inter-
penetrating all is the manifold beauty of sea and sky, and the
imagination-teasing, distant presence of the lighthouse itself. It has
been observed that it is both a male and a female symbol: phallic,
and a lonely image of male destiny to James and his father; caressing
and bringing ecstatic inner fulfilment to Mrs Ramsay. The lighthouse
is of course more than this, like all poetic symbols of great power
which can be felt but never fully explained by the analytical mind.
Virginia herself knew this, as her letter to Roger Fry, when he

Leonard Woolf at Cassis

complained that the symbolism escaped him, makes crystal clear. 'I meant *nothing* by the lighthouse,' she wrote. 'I can't manage symbolism except in this vague, generalised way. Whether it's right or wrong I don't know; but directly I'm told what a thing means, it becomes hateful to me.'

It became the pattern of Virginia Woolf's writing to follow one of her major, poetic novels with a 'novel of fact', as she followed *The Voyage Out* with *Night and Day*; or with what she called a 'holiday' book. This was partly due to her need to relax from her supreme visionary efforts, which so often brought her to the edge of breakdown and madness, partly also because she was aware of possessing a multiplicity of gifts; of being able, as she wrote in her diary, to write 'books that relieve other books: a variety of styles and subjects: for after all that is my temperament'.

After finishing *To the Lighthouse*, she in fact wrote two books to relieve the dangerous tension in her mind that had once more arisen in the last stages. 'I feel the need', she noted, 'of an escapade after these serious poetic experimental books whose form is always so closely considered. I want to kick up my heels and be off.' One of these two was *A Room of One's Own*; the other, the earlier, *Orlando*, was a true 'holiday' book, the writing of which appeared to cause her immense happiness from the beginning to the end – or very nearly to the end, for she never finished any book without some sensation of rising anxiety.

By the time she had published *Monday or Tuesday* and *Jacob's Room*, her growing recognition as an original artist was bringing her an ever-widening circle of new friends and admirers. One of them was Vita Sackville-West, the wife of a young diplomatist, Harold Nicolson. Both had a deep interest in literature, and both had started on writing careers of their own. They met Virginia at a dinner-party given by Clive Bell in 1922. Vita was descended from an ancient aristocratic family and had been brought up at Knole, one of the more famous stately homes of England. Vita had a striking presence and beauty, to which the blood of her Spanish grandmother added a special exotic flavour. She had two sons by Harold Nicolson, but her predominant sexual tastes were lesbian, as his were also for his own sex; in fact by 1922 the marriage, except as a deep and lasting companionship, appears to have been already over.

All this, we must presume, Virginia was aware of. She was not particularly impressed at the first meeting, or so her diary entries would lead one to believe. 'Not much to my severe taste,' she noted, 'florid, moustached, parakeet coloured, with all the supple ease of the aristocracy, but not the wit of the artist.' But Vita was impressed with Virginia, found her beautiful, desirable, and immensely fascinating

Vita Sackville-West in 1924

Harold Nicolson, diplomatist and author, husband of Vita Sackville-West

as a mind; recognizing at once, one cannot help feeling, that she had intellectual qualities superior to her own.

Virginia had already shown herself capable of strong emotional attachments to women in her relationships with Madge Vaughan and Violet Dickinson in her youth (and to a limited extent with Katherine Mansfield later); but one must conclude from all the evidence we have that she had made up her mind that her marriage to Leonard Woolf came unalterably first, even though her feeling for Vanessa was probably even stronger. Nevertheless, what one can only describe as a love-affair developed between Virginia and Vita in the years that followed. Early on, in 1924, Vita had an intuition about the reality of their relationship. 'Look on it,' she wrote to Virginia, 'if you like, as copy – as I believe you do on everything, human relationships included. Oh yes, you like people better through the brain than through the heart.' It was a stinging accusation, for Virginia showed all the signs of an anxious lover, at one moment despair at absence or neglect, at the next joy at reunion or the arrival of letters full of love, and admitted that Vita's emotion for her 'excites and flatters and interests'; but deep down, I believe, Virginia was not deceived, either by herself or by Vita, nor did she bemuse herself into seeing Vita's poetry in anything but an austere critical light; and the affair did become copy for a book: *Orlando*.

At the beginning of October 1927, she writes in her diary that she is free for the moment of journalistic work. 'And instantly the usual exciting devices enter my mind: a biography beginning in the year 1500 and continuing to the present day, called *Orlando*: Vita; only with a change about from one sex to another. I think, for a treat, I shall let myself dash this in for a week.' Little more than two weeks later she comments on those last words and writes: 'I have done nothing, nothing, nothing else for a fortnight; and am launched somewhat furtively but with all the more passion upon *Orlando*: a Biography. . . . I walk making up phrases; sit, contriving scenes; am in short in the thick of the greatest rapture known to me, from which I have kept myself since last February, or earlier. . . . But the balance between truth and fantasy must be careful.' On Sunday, 18 March of the following year, she announces that '*Orlando* was finished yesterday as the clock struck one. Anyhow, the canvas is covered. There will be three months of close work needed, imperatively, before it can be printed.' But in fact she did her revising in very much less time (and that time included a motoring holiday abroad), and by 31 March writes that Leonard (who was always the first to see her final corrected typescripts) had given his essential approval, and was in fact more enthusiastic than she expected. Her mind, almost incredibly, was already gestating a new novel, which was to turn out to be *The Waves*. On the eve of *Orlando*'s publication she went away alone with Vita for a week in France, to Paris and Burgundy; and eventually presented her with the manuscript.

Virginia was well aware that *Orlando* was not the kind of book on which a great literary reputation would rest; though I think she was also aware that in its own genre it was very good and (as Leonard agreed) extremely original. 'I never got down to my depths', she wrote in her diary in November, after publication and success, 'and made shapes square up, as I did in the *Lighthouse*'; but immediately after, '*Orlando* was the outcome of a perfectly definite, indeed over-mastering impulse. I want fun. I want fantasy.' The fun and the fantasy start the moment one opens the book, with the spoof acknow-ledgments in the Preface, in which she thanks every single one of her friends, most of whom could not possibly have had any hand in the work, including a 'gentleman in America' whose name and address she had lost, 'who had generously and gratuitously corrected the punctuation, the botany, the entomology, the geography, and the chronology of previous works of mine, and will, I hope, not spare

Detail from a painting of the two sons of the fourth Earl of Dorset, at Knole, used by Virginia Woolf to illustrate 'Orlando as a boy'

'Orlando about the year 1840', from *Orlando, A Biography*, 1928. It is in fact a photograph of Vita Sackville-West in fancy dress

Virginia Woolf in a photograph by Man Ray, *c.* 1927

his services on the present occasion'. The illustrations are also an elaborate joke, perhaps perilously near an in-joke: three of the pictures of *Orlando* are photographs of Vita, and the picture of the Russian princess as a child is a photograph of Angelica Bell in fancy-dress. From the very first pages every rule of probability and verisimilitude is broken, and throughout the book a continuous fountain of fantastic images and wildly improbable situations pours out; it never seems to fail, nor do the wit and the gaiety. As she was writing it, she declared that she wanted it to be 'half laughing, half serious, with great splashes of exaggeration'. The exaggeration is certainly everywhere: for instance, history does not recognize any feature of the Great Frost of King James I's reign as extravagant as Virginia presents us with in her celebrated description, such as the picture of the wrecked wherry boat 'plainly visible, lying on the bed of the river where it had sunk last autumn, overladen with apples', with the bumboat woman who 'sat

Aerial view of Knole, ancestral home of the Sackvilles

there in her plaids and farthingales with her lap full of apples, for all the world as if she were about to serve a customer'.

After the Great Frost, perhaps the most impressive and beautiful of the descriptions in *Orlando* are of the great house, more a town than a family dwelling, plainly modelled on Knole. Virginia was here giving rein to the fascination she had always had, not only with ancestral houses, great or small, but also with the panorama of English history, an obsessive delight that comes out again and again in her critical writings and in her final phase, in the posthumous novel, *Between the Acts*; and could be fully indulged in here, as Orlando is ageless and presented as existing through all periods from the Elizabethan to the twentieth century.

The Venetian Ambassador's room at Knole

The other most striking aspect of *Orlando* is, of course, her treatment of the theme of androgyny, clearly inspired by Vita's flamboyant impulse to change from female dress into male dress, and even, at one time, appear in the streets of London as a wounded young officer. Not only does Orlando change from man to woman in the middle of the book, but the absurd Archduchess Harriet Griselda appears love-lorn for Orlando when he is a man, and equally lovelorn, but as an Archduke (which it is suggested he has been all along), when Orlando has been metamorphosed into a woman. And at the end, when Orlando and Marmaduke Bonthrop Shelmerdine fall in love with one another, each is constantly suspecting the other of being of the opposite sex to that professed. This theme of androgyny had occupied

Aphra Behn

Jane Austen, by Cassandra Austen

George Eliot, by F. d'Albert-Durade

Virginia's mind for many years, and indeed makes a muted appearance as early as *The Voyage Out*. It was to assume a much more important place in her next book, *A Room of One's Own*.

In October 1928 Virginia Woolf gave two lectures in Cambridge colleges, one to the Arts Society at Newnham, and the other to a similar society at Girton, on 'Women and Fiction', and it was out of these lectures (which she said were too long in any case to be read in full) that she constructed *A Room of One's Own*, published as a separate book the following year. Basically, it is a polemic on the inferior status of women that has persisted in European civilization from the earliest times to the present day. Virginia admits the gradual erosion of inequality and prejudice in her own time, but insists that it still has a very long way to go, and that the idea of the inferiority of women is still deeply rooted in men's minds. Specifically, it is a claim that 'a woman must have money and a room of her own if she is to write fiction', and it is argued with the most remarkable force and the most telling illustrative examples. And yet rarely, if ever, was a polemic delivered or a claim upheld with such good humour, such wit, such imaginative illumination or such absence of rancorous rhetoric. And it is not only about the status of women, but also about the creative intelligence, the nature of genius, and the doom of Fascism. It is spirited, lucid, cogent, amusing; it is, in fact, a masterpiece.

Virginia takes us on a series of excursions and reflections in six chapters. In the first, we are in Cambridge (she calls it Oxbridge, but it is perfectly obvious from the start that we are, in fact, in her beloved Cambridge), and she notes with sly exactitude the difference between the luxurious appurtenances of life in a man's college, where she is feasted with the most delicious of luncheons (and forbidden as a woman to enter the famous Library without special introduction), and the measly supper she is offered at the women's college she visits in the evening. In the next chapter, we are in the British Museum, where she finds an enormous number of books by men about women, and in particular one by a Professor von X (who stands for a whole phalanx of woman-despisers) on *The Mental, Moral, and Physical Inferiority of the Female Sex*, and makes fun of him for his anger, which she feels betrays his insecurity as a member of the dominant sex. That England is under the rule of a patriarchy is proved by a glance at the evening paper; she then informs us that she has been left £500 a year by an aunt, and how that completely changes her woman's condition. In the third chapter she imagines what would have happened to a sister of Shakespeare, if he had had one with the same gifts as his own; how she would have been forced to deny her gifts and remain silent

and subservient her whole life through. In the fourth chapter, she traces the gradual emergence of women writers, and the enormous difficulty they found in the earlier centuries of our literature, until, with Aphra Behn in the late seventeenth century, a corner is at last turned. She made money by her writing, and Virginia sees that fact as the beginning of female liberation; yet even in the nineteenth century, when the great women novelists appear, she observes that they had – with the unique exception of Jane Austen – to camouflage themselves with men's names, George Eliot, Currer, Ellis and Acton Bell. In this chapter she makes two very striking statements. One is about the necessity of women writers to find a sentence that will express themselves, and not to borrow the male sentence which expresses such an entirely different temperament; one can say that all her writing life Virginia was in search of such a sentence. The other statement is about genius. Discussing *War and Peace*, she says: 'One holds every phrase, every scene to the light as one reads – for Nature seems, very oddly, to have provided us with an inner light by which to judge of the novelist's integrity or disintegrity. Or perhaps it is rather that Nature, in her most irrational mood, has traced in invisible ink on the walls of the mind a

Jane Ellen Harrison, by Augustus John; '. . . a bent figure, formidable yet humble, with her great forehead and her shabby dress – could it be the famous scholar, could it be J— H— herself?' From *A Room of One's Own*

Emily Brontë, by Branwell Brontë

premonition which these great artists confirm; a sketch which only needs to be held to the fire of genius to become visible.'

The fifth chapter is important, because in it Virginia makes absolutely clear that she does not want women to be like men; she does not advocate anything remotely like the modern conception of the blurring of the sexes; in fact she thinks that women should *fortify the differences* between themselves and men, for only thus can they come into their own. And she paints a picture, remarkable for a childless woman, of how a woman has always been able to stimulate and encourage man in his career or creativity: 'He would open the door of drawing-room or nursery, I thought, and find her among her children perhaps, or with a piece of embroidery on her knee – at any rate, the centre of some different order and system of life.'

When it comes to writing, however, she has, in her last chapter, something rather different to say: she believes, with Coleridge, that the creative mind of the poet or novelist should be androgynous; that if there are two sexes of the body, there are also two sexes of the mind, but frequently inhabiting the same body, whether male or female; and that the best writing is produced when the man (or the woman) allows these two sexes to collaborate:

And I went on amateurishly to sketch a plan of the soul so that in each of us two powers preside, one male, one female; and in the man's brain, the man predominates over the woman, and in the woman's brain, the woman predominates over the man. The normal and comfortable state of being is that when the two live in harmony together, spiritually co-operating. If one is a man, still the woman part of the brain must have effect; and a woman also must have intercourse with the man in her. Coleridge perhaps meant this when he said that a great mind is androgynous. It is when this fusion takes place that the mind is fully fertilised and uses all its faculties. Perhaps a mind that is purely masculine cannot create, any more than a mind that is purely feminine, I thought.

In her final pages Virginia Woolf makes her most uncompromising declaration about the task of the artist, a declaration that casts a light over the whole of her life, and can only bring a feeling of humility to any writer less dedicated:

So long as you write what you wish to write, that is all that matters; and whether it matters for ages or only for hours, nobody can say. But to sacrifice a hair of the head of your vision, a shade of its colour, in deference to some Headmaster with a silver pot in his hand or to some professor with a measuring-rod up his sleeve, is the most abject treachery, and the sacrifice of wealth and chastity, which used to be said to be the greatest of human disasters, a mere flea-bite in comparison.

If one stops to consider Virginia Woolf's situation, as a writer and as a human being, at the beginning of the year 1930, when she was already hard at work on the novel that many people think her supreme

Samuel Taylor Coleridge, by Washington Allston, 1814

achievement, *The Waves*, one is struck at once by the great changes that had taken place in it in the course of the previous decade. She had, during the 1920s, step by step built up her reputation as an original and experimental novelist, and had gradually increased her sales as the literary world began to realize how important it was to have read the 'latest Virginia Woolf', even though to many readers her method and intentions were still baffling. But *Orlando* made her a best-seller. It was easy to read, deliciously light-hearted and fantastical; and slightly scandalous. A third edition was ordered within a few months of publication, and before Christmas 1928 more than six thousand copies had been sold. She records in her diary: 'For the first time since I married, 1912–1928 – 16 years, I have been spending money. The spending muscle does not work naturally yet. I feel guilty; put off buying, when I know that I should buy; and yet have an agreeable luxurious sense of coins in my pocket beyond my weekly 13/– which was always running out, or being encroached upon.' And in January 1930 she finds that she 'had made about £3,020 last year – the salary of a civil servant: a surprise to me, who was content with £200 for so many years'. A month later she records that *A Room of One's Own* had sold ten thousand copies, which promised further financial ease for the future. And this sale referred only to the British edition: her sales in America were going up all the time, almost one may say by leaps and bounds. One presumes that when she speaks of £3,020, she is referring only to her earnings from royalties and possibly also her fees for articles; but there was in addition her profit from the Hogarth Press, in which she was still a half-sharer. Thus Virginia earned double from her writings, as author and publisher; the long uphill road was leading at last to a plateau of comfort, if not of luxury. But one must enter a word of caution here. Leonard was always very canny about money, and meticulous in his calculations. He had instituted a system by which all their earnings were pooled. Out of this pool all expenses were paid, and the rest was divided between them equally, into separate 'hoards'. As Virginia's earnings from 1928 onwards were enormously greater than Leonard's (mainly derived from his journalism and books, his literary editorship of the *Nation* and subsequent joint-editorship of the *Political Quarterly*), the equal division meant that (after tax) of those large earnings in the year 1929 she only had just over £1,000 in her own 'hoard'.

In any case, they could now buy all sorts of things that had seemed to them distant luxuries in the early years of their marriage: a car, in which on several occasions they made trips abroad, new furniture for Monk's House, to which they made additions and improvements, books and pictures. Virginia was so curiously unconcerned about dress that it seems unlikely that much of her 'hoard' was spent on her wardrobe.

Virginia Woolf with her niece
Angelica, Vanessa Bell's daughter,
and a small bird, *c.* 1932

It is interesting to note that the pattern of writing which was
forced on her by her delicate health was at the same time the luckiest
for her reputation. It was the 'holiday' books she wrote in between her
major novels that brought her the ever-widening popularity which was
then reflected in the sales of her subsequent books. But this new ease
did not mean any respite from the demon that drove her. She adored
her nephews and nieces and was immensely popular with them. Their
father, Clive Bell, has written that they enjoyed beyond anything a
visit from Virginia, and looked forward to it as the greatest treat
imaginable. 'Virginia's coming, what fun we shall have!' She hated
to miss one of their parties, in which compositions of their own were
produced, fancy-dress often donned – in one of them held about this
time all the guests were disguised as characters from *Alice in Wonderland*
– and Virginia herself could sometimes be persuaded to take the floor
with a song. Nevertheless, she could write in her diary, after one of
these parties, in December 1927:

The little creatures acting moved my infinitely sentimental throat. Angelica so mature and composed; all grey and silver; such an epitome of all womanliness; and such an unopened bud of sense and sensibility; wearing a grey wig and a sea-coloured dress. And yet oddly enough I scarcely want children of my own now. This insatiable desire to write something before I die, this ravaging sense of the shortness and feverishness of life, make me cling, like a man on a rock, to my one anchor. I don't like the physicalness of having children of one's own. This occurred to me at Rodmell; but I never wrote it down. I can dramatise myself a parent, it is true. And perhaps I have killed the feeling instinctively; or perhaps nature does.

One of the liveliest and most interesting of these parties took place in January 1935 in Vanessa's studio at 8 Fitzroy Street, when a performance was given of *Freshwater*, a play which Virginia had originally written twelve years before but had since completely revised. It dealt with the life of Julia Margaret Cameron, Virginia's great-aunt and famous early photographer, and her friends on the Isle of Wight. Vanessa herself took the part of Mrs Cameron, her husband was

72

Virginia Woolf with Quentin Bell, c. 1924

played by Leonard, Tennyson by Julian Bell, Ellen Terry by Angelica and G. F. Watts by Duncan Grant. It appears to have amused Clive Bell and his brother so much that their roars of laughter all but drowned the dialogue.

If Virginia profited, in more ways than merely financial, from the existence of the Hogarth Press, it had nevertheless become a source of worry and exasperation as well as of pride, and was demanding too much of their time. It was successful; it had published, after the

(*Opposite*)
Clive Bell and his family (Julian, Quentin, Angelica); painting by Vanessa Bell, 1924

The first treadle printing machine for the Hogarth Press, now at Sissinghurst

The covers of a Hogarth Press pamphlet and the complete catalogue of 1939, designed by Vanessa Bell

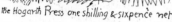

Walter Sickert: a conversation. By Virginia Woolf.

the Hogarth Press one shilling & sixpence net

Complete Catalogue of the Hogarth Press

dazzling first three years of the little books printed by the Woolfs themselves, which are now so famous and so rare, a large number of books by outstanding writers of the day, many of them of or close to Bloomsbury; it had a distinguished name for its poetry above all, for its *avant-garde* fiction and its books and pamphlets of literary, artistic and political criticism. Works by Svevo, Bunin and Rilke headed its pioneering translations. It had taken on a brilliant iconoclastic young novelist and poet from South Africa, William Plomer; and was soon to take on the young Christopher Isherwood;

in 1930 it had published Vita Sackville-West's most successful novel, *The Edwardians*, after several travel books; and it had the solid commercial base not only of Virginia's books but also of Freud's, and other psychoanalytical works. At the same time, it has to be admitted that in too many cases it failed to keep its authors, the cause of which appears to have been more than anything else a flaw in Leonard's temperament. He was determined – one can only call it that – to keep the Press going on a shoe-string. The basement of 52 Tavistock Square, where the Press conducted its activities, was in a state of dilapidation. The windows did not open properly, the toilet was inadequately furnished, the heating was primitive. It was always understaffed, and Leonard could never bring himself to employ a professional traveller. The production was often skimped and depressingly utility. Little wonder, then, that it was easy for agents to suggest to an author, after he had made his first success under the Hogarth imprint, that the sales potentiality of his books would never be properly exploited until he moved to a firm with a fully developed publishing machine – and a readiness to give him better terms. This did not matter in the case of Virginia's books, when her name was on everyone's lips; but it *did* matter for the young at the start of their writing careers. It was ironical, perhaps, but it was inevitable.

Christopher Isherwood, *c.* 1936

These inadequacies were made worse by the depressing tale of the young men Leonard engaged as managers. One after another they passed through the work-room at Hogarth House or the basement at Tavistock Square, eager to learn the mysteries of publishing and excited to be working with a firm of such high literary reputation; one after another they left, all ardour spent, after a few years or even a few months. It was not so much that they were expected to do a dozen menial jobs, such as doing up parcels and running round to the post, as well as to become experts at book-keeping, designing advertisements, ordering paper of the right size, weight and texture in the correct amounts, sending out review copies and chasing up the booksellers, interviewing the bores and the lunatics, and machining labels and stationery in the printing-press scullery, all without any previous experience. After all, Leonard took a hand in most of this himself, and even Virginia would help with the parcels when there was a rush. The trouble was much more that with each of these young men Leonard, after a honeymoon period of a few weeks when he would induct them into their manifold obligations with fatherly patience and humour, would become increasingly impatient, intolerant of little mistakes, and testy – indeed often hysterically angry – when things were not going quite to his liking; and when he was testy he could be extremely rude. The result was that each attempt to lift the burden on to a young man's shoulders ended in more time wasted, mainly in altercation and nerves frayed all round. Virginia ostensibly

William Plomer, 1948

The two Hogarth Press colophons

75

Lytton Strachey with his friend
Ralph Partridge

dissociated herself from these disputes, and tried every now and then to lower the temperature with a little gesture of appeasement; but behind the scenes she was almost always on Leonard's side, perhaps wanting a quiet life above all, perhaps truly believing in his impeccable wisdom. Ralph Partridge, Lytton Strachey's friend, was the first of these young men; he was followed by George (Dadie) Rylands, who stayed only six months before being saved by a Fellowship at King's College, Cambridge, though he remained a lifelong friend of the Woolfs; then came Angus Davidson, who was to make an out-standing reputation as a translator from Italian. He lasted for the record period of three years, but in the end the rows were too much for him too. The next was a very young man, Richard Kennedy, who has produced an extremely funny illustrated account of his brief apprenticeship. In 1930, the job was vacant again, and the Woolfs thought seriously of giving up the Press; but they eventually recruited the present writer, who was at the Press during the last stages of the writing of *The Waves*, and its publication.

The Waves was already hovering at the back of Virginia's mind as early as June 1927, but at that period, and for some time to come, she called it *The Moths*, and in her diary it appears as a very different book from what it eventually became. In November 1928, however, she makes an important note about the way she wants to write it: 'I mean to eliminate all waste, deadness, superfluity: to give the moment whole; whatever it includes. Say that the moment is a combination of thought; sensation; the voice of the sea. . . . This appalling narrative business of the realist: getting on from lunch to dinner: it is false, unreal, merely

Virginia Woolf and John Lehmann at Rodmell, in 1931, photographed by Leonard Woolf

conventional. Why admit anything to literature that is not poetry – by which I mean saturated? . . . That is what I want to do in *The Moths*.' Not until nearly a year later does the idea of calling the book *The Waves* enter her head; and she gives a rather comic reason, or part-reason, for the change of title: 'Moths, I suddenly remember, don't fly by day.' In September 1929 the real work starts, but the beginning proves difficult; on Boxing Day she records: 'I write two pages of arrant nonsense, after straining; I write variations of every sentence; compromises; bad shots; possibilities; till my writing book is like a lunatic's dream.' By the middle of January it is beginning to flow, and in April she has actually finished the first revision. Finally, on 7 February 1931, she announces the end of the second version in a crucial note: 'I must record, heaven be praised, the end of *The Waves*. I wrote the last words O Death fifteen minutes ago, having reeled across the last ten pages with some moments of such

(*Opposite left*) George (Dadie) Rylands at Monk's House, in a photograph by Leonard Woolf

(*Opposite right*) Angus Davidson, in a photograph by Leonard Woolf

77

perceive then, you & I, road & I, horse & rider
on we stand pawing the pavement?
O death! ~~You~~ You are the
means. You are my final
offering. You are the horrible
presence against which I will
ride with my spear
couched, with my hair
flung back like a young
man, like Percival
when he galloped ~~in~~
~~to~~ & like him I will
fling myself against you,
~~'tis~~ unvanquished, unyielding
O death.

Saturday | Feb. 7th 1931

intensity and intoxication that I seemed only to stumble after my own voice, or almost, after some sort of speaker (as when I was mad). I was almost afraid, remembering the voices that used to fly ahead.'

That note was uncomfortably prophetic. She had still to revise the second version, to type it out and correct the typescript; and then came the proofs to be corrected in their turn. The effort and the tension were terrific. The headaches began again and Leonard, in a state of acute anxiety, ordered her to drop the work and rest completely. She recovered, and when she had finished the final version Leonard, always the first to see her completed work, declared it was a master-piece. This gave a much-needed boost to her morale, but the headaches came on once more when the proofs were corrected and the always dangerous interval of waiting for the actual publication arrived. It seems to have been touch and go. The first letter she had about it, from Hugh Walpole who had seen an advance copy, plunged her into gloom: he could hardly understand a word. Very soon after, however, letters of praise and enthusiasm began to come in. In a mood now transformed, she wrote a revealing reply to one of these enthusiasts, perhaps the youngest, in which she described something of her aims: 'It was, I think, a difficult attempt – I wanted to eliminate all detail; all fact; and analysis; and myself; and yet not be frigid and rhetorical; and not monotonous (which I am) and to keep the swiftness of prose and yet strike one or two sparks, and not with poetical, but pure-bred prose, and keep the elements of character; and yet that there should be many characters and only one; and also an infinity, a background behind – well, I admit I was biting off too much.'

The Waves was indeed, as she had described it at an early stage, 'a completely new attempt', as well as a 'different attempt', and more ambitious than anything she had set her hand to before. Her aim, one can say, was to give a picture of the whole of life from the earliest dawning of sensation to the end; of its dreams, ambitions, aspirations, achievements and failures, to its final disillusionments, accompanied perhaps by acceptance or the joyous discovery of wisdom. More completely than ever before, it is the life of the soul she is giving us, stripping away everything that could encumber or obscure that vision. And, restless as ever to find new, more perfect ways of showing us *her* reality, she invents an entirely new technique, which makes *The Waves* as different from *To the Lighthouse* and *Mrs Dalloway* as those two novels are from *The Voyage Out*.

The structure, to begin with, has become entirely formal, and the narrative totally internalized. She takes six characters, three male and three female, and traces their lives through nine episodes, prefaced and separated by short descriptive interludes, in which the sun rises on a garden by the seashore and sets at the close; but the sunset is not only the end of the day but also the end of a year, so that the action is

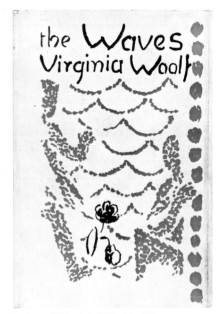

Jacket of Virginia Woolf's *The Waves*, designed by Vanessa Bell, 1931

(*Opposite*) The last page of the manuscript of *The Waves*

divided symbolically not merely by times of day but by seasons of the year as well. And behind everything are the waves, image of eternal recurrence, of the heartbeat of the universe. These interludes are purely descriptive and the only objectively descriptive passages in the book. Everything else is soliloquy: the characters speak their thoughts aloud (if you can call it that) in turn, at each successive period in their lives, and are always, even in childhood, entirely articulate and self-aware. Thus all the trappings of realism are finally discarded, and a new, highly artificial convention developed, that may remind one more of classical drama than the novel. The prose, except in the final summing-up soliloquy by Bernard, has lost some of the outstanding speed of the two earlier novels; in its place it has a strong underlying beat, which might indeed tremble on the verge of monotony, as she feared, if it were not for subtle variations and changes of rhythm from time to time. The formal structure is certainly partly responsible for making the book harder to read, but what is also partly, and perhaps even more responsible is the dazzling concentration of imagery throughout, illuminating a movement of thought that has become of the most intricate complexity.

Each character is given his or her descriptive 'label' or theme tune, which is repeated in variations throughout the book. It is as if Virginia Woolf were insisting that in certain basic traits human beings, once formed, do not change during their lives, even though the dominant traits may be to some extent modified by the impact of other human beings or by one circumstance or another. And these traits are shown to be, in many cases, at least partly the result of traumatic disturbances in childhood, as when Susan sees Jinny kiss Louis, and Neville on the stairs hears tell of the man lying with his throat cut under the 'immitigable apple tree'. Nevertheless, we see them gradually differentiated as they grow up, and, in their own soliloquies and as reflected in the thoughts of the others, changing, as they are shadowed by death and loss, by their growing awareness that certain ambitions and dreams will never be fulfilled and by the disappointments of advancing age. To mark and emphasize these changes, Virginia brings them all together on two occasions; first at a farewell dinner to Percival, the silent focus of love and admiration, who by the time of the next episode has met his death in India – Percival, shadow-figure created from Virginia's ever-fresh memory of her brother Thoby, who 'was flowering with green leaves and was laid in the earth with all his branches still sighing in the summer wind'; and at the end, in the evening of their lives, at a reunion dinner at Hampton Court.

To Bernard, in the coda, is allotted the task of the utmost difficulty, but crucial to Virginia's design, of giving an interpretation of the adventure of all their lives: 'What a symphony with its concord and its discord, and its tunes on top and its complicated bass beneath!'

(*Opposite*) A page from Virginia Woolf's diary referring to the preparation of *The Waves*, then called *The Moths*, 28 November 1928

(*Overleaf*) Letter about *The Waves* from Virginia Woolf to John Lehmann, 17 September 1931

of them ought to be possible.   The idea has come to me
that what I want now to do is to saturate every
atom. I mean to eliminate all waste, deadness,
superfluity: to give the moment whole; whatever
whatever it includes.   Say that the moment
is a combination of thought; sensation; the voice of the sea.
Waste, deadness, come from the inclusion of things
that don't belong to the moment; this appalling
narrative business of the realist: getting on from
lunch to dinner: it is false, unreal, merely
conventional.   Why admit anything to
literature that is not poetry — by which I mean
saturated? Is that not my grudge against novelists? ?

at they
select nothing?

The poets succeed usually by succeeding by
simplifying: practically everything is left out. I
want to put practically everything in; yet to saturate.
That is what I want to do in The Moths.
It must include nonsense. fact, sordidity: but
made transparent.   I think I must read Ibsen
Shakespeare. & Racine.   And I will write
something about them; for that is the best spur,
my mind. being what it is; then I read with
fury & gusto. Otherwise I skip & skip: I am a
lazy reader.   But no: I am surprised & a
little disquieted by the remorseless severity of my
mind: that it never stops reading & writing;
makes me write on Geraldine Jewsbury, on
Hardy, on Women — is this professional,
is this living any longer a dreamy amateur

Monks House   Sept 17th
Rodmell.

Dear John,

I'm most grateful to you for your letter. It
made me happy all yesterday. I had become
firmly convinced that the Waves was a failure,
in the sense that it wouldn't convey anything to
anybody. And now you've been so perceptive,
& gone so much further & deeper in understanding
my drift than I thought possible that I'm
immensely relieved.   Not that I expect many such
readers. And I'm rather dismayed to hear we've
printed 7,000: for I'm sure 3,000 will
feed feed all such appetites; & then the other 4
will sit round me like decaying corpses for ever
in the studio (I cleared up the table — for John, not
the corpses)   I agree that its very difficult —
bristling with horrors, though I've never worked so
hard as I did here, to smoothing them out. But it
was, I think, a difficult attempt — I wanted to
eliminate all detail; all fact; & analysis;
& my self; & yet not be jejune &
rhetorical; & not monotonous (which I am)

& to keep the swiftness of prose & yet strike one or two
sparks, & not <s>be</s> wholly poetical, but pure fired prose, &
yet keep the elements of character; & <s>feel</s> feel that there
should be many characters, & only one; & also an immensity, a background
behind <s>back ground</s> — Well, I admit I was biting off too much.

But enough, as the poets say. If I
live another 50 years I think I shall put this
method to some use, but as in 50 years I
shall be under the pond, with the gold fish swimming
over me, I daresay these vast ambitions <s>are</s> are a
little foolish, & will ruin the press. That
reminds me — I think your idea of a Letter most
brilliant — <s>To</s> To a Young Poet: because I'm seething
with immature & ill considered & wild &
annoying ideas about prose & poetry. So
lend me your name — (& let me sketch a
character of the by way of frontispiece) — & then I'll
pour forth all I can think of about you young, &
we old, & novels — how damned they are — & poetry,
how dead. But I must take a look into the
subject. & you must reply, "To an old novelist" —
I must read Auden, whom I've not read, & Spender (his novel
I swear I will tackle tonight). The whole subject is
crying out for letters — flocks. volleys. of them. from
every side. Why not get Spender & Auden &
the Day Lewis to join in? But you must
go to Miss Belsher. & I must go to my luncheon.
This is only a scribble to say how grateful
I am for your letter.
Yr Virginia Woolf

Again and again, as he sums the story up, he has the mystical sense of losing his precise identity, even, Tiresias-like, his sex: 'It is not one life that I look back upon; I am not one person; I am many people . . . nor do I always know if I am man or woman, Bernard or Neville, Louis, Susan, Jinny or Rhoda – so strange is the contact of one with another.' Particularly evocative is his use of two symbols that appear to have haunted Virginia's imagination: the tree – here a willow tree – that stands for something enduring in life, 'the tree alone resisted our eternal flux', a symbol that recurs in book after book, most powerfully perhaps in *Orlando*, whose poem, one remembers, was called 'The Oak Tree'; and, far stranger, the image of 'a fin' that rises in the wastes of silence, a symbol that seems to have been mysteriously charged with meaning for Virginia. It was the result, it would appear, of an actual moment of mystical vision, for when she records in her diary the completion of *The Waves*, she writes: 'I mean that I have netted that fin in the waste of water which appeared to me over the marshes out of my window at Rodmell when I was coming to an end of *To the Lighthouse*.'

One other image, or episode, surprisingly rarely remarked upon by the critics, seems by its recurrence in Bernard's summing-up, and the way it recurs, clearly to have been intended by Virginia to bear a special significance. In their childhood, Bernard escapes with Susan

The Farm Pond near Firle, Sussex; painting by Duncan Grant, 1930–32

to a secret vantage-point in the depths of the woods – described in a way that suggests rather a vision or dream than an actual place – from which they can see a 'great house' far beneath them, ringed by a wall that protects it from the rest of the world – and from time: 'Now we wake the sleeping daws who have never seen a human form; now we tread on rotten oak apples, red with age and slippery.' Within the wall is a garden, where 'the gardeners sweep the lawn with giant brooms', and would, Bernard imagines, shoot him and Susan like jays if they espied them. They can see the roofs of the house, and a stable clock 'with its gilt hands shining'; and, between two long windows in the house, a lady writing. Virginia does not give us any further clues; but it is hardly possible to escape the conclusion that she intends the 'lady writing' as an image of the artist at her task beyond time and contingency. And this conclusion is reinforced by Bernard's first recalling of the image in his summing-up:

On the outskirts of every agony sits some observant fellow who points; who whispers as he whispered to me that summer morning in the house where the corn comes up to the windows, 'The willow grows on the turf by the river. The gardeners sweep with great brooms and the lady sits writing.' Thus he directed me to that which is beyond and outside our own predicament; to that which is symbolic, and thus perhaps permanent, if there is any permanence in our sleeping, eating, breathing, so animal, so spiritual and tumultuous lives.

It is impossible in a brief summary to do justice to the visionary insights of the book, or to the immense richness, power and distinction of the prose, or to the splendour of the final passage where Bernard rides against death. It has been objected that, for a picture of the whole of life, it is a fault that sexual passion is absent. Certainly the physical description of passion is absent; but the importance and physicality of marriage, child-bearing and child-rearing in the life of Susan is clearly brought out, as is the fact that Jinny only lives in the light of the sexual admiration of men, and Neville for the intimacy of the young men he desires. In *To the Lighthouse* Virginia Woolf had shown her vision of 'being in love' – the engagement of Paul and Minta – as a savage blaze of fire; for the depiction of the power of lust, we must wait for Virginia Woolf's last phase. It has also been objected that, for such a fun-loving, witty and even at times malicious person as Virginia undoubtedly was, comedy is curiously absent. One should, however, not forget the deliciously comic portrait of the headmaster of the boys' school, nor the continual touches of absurdity with which Bernard's character is built up. But the truth is that Virginia, who could display the most delicate sense of comedy when she wished, as many passages in the 'holiday' books and the critical essays show, when she wrote her serious novels was controlled by a deeper, more tragic emotion. When she was at work on *To the Lighthouse*, she noted in her diary: 'I have an idea that I will invent a new name for my books to supplant "novel". A new . . . by Virginia Woolf. But what? Elegy?'

As her fame increased, Virginia began to be offered lectures, visits to the United States and public honours. She rejected almost all of them. She refused to be made a Companion of·Honour or to accept a Doctorate from Manchester University. She was invited to give the Clark Lectures at Cambridge in 1932, and turned the offer down (though with misgivings, thinking how proud her father would have been). She never went to the United States. At the same time, she inevitably attracted to herself a cloud of new fans, lion-hunters like the society hostesses Lady Colefax and Lady Cunard, but many of them, like Vita, creative artists themselves, novelists, poets, musicians. One of the most persistent and unsnubbable was Hugh Walpole, whose letter of incomprehension about *The Waves* has already been mentioned. He adored her, though so often baffled by her work; and Virginia, for her part, enjoyed his adoration and would tease him affectionately, though she put no high estimate on his novels and could laugh at him behind his back. She often acted as his confidante, the recipient of many confessions about the secret part of his life, his homosexual infatuations. Virginia's enormous curiosity about other people's lives, and her total lack of sexual prejudice, made her an ideal mother-confessor; and for this, one judges, he was profoundly grateful and could forgive or ignore what he must have suspected was her opinion of his work.

Hugh Walpole, devoted admirer of Virginia Woolf

Just about the time when she was deeply occupied with her work on *The Waves*, at the beginning of 1930, an even more unsnubbable and demanding fan appeared. 'An old woman of seventy-one has fallen in love with me,' Virginia wrote. 'It's like being caught by a giant crab.'

The 'giant crab' was Dame Ethel Smyth, composer and indomitable personality of crackling vitality. For a time she wrote to Virginia twice a day. She would arrive at the house in Tavistock Square, like a battleship with all guns firing, plunge into the studio where Virginia was working, and totally disrupt that work. Virginia was once more amused and flattered, and perhaps flirted a little with the new, devouring worshipper; but Ethel Smyth's remorseless love soon became too much for her, and the honeymoon period lasted little more than a few months. Thereafter they remained friends, but wary. Perfervid though the emotions were that Virginia aroused in her, Ethel Smyth was no fool; and when the blaze of love cooled, she could find fault with Virginia as sharply as Virginia could with her. Nevertheless, much of her criticism of Virginia, on political and religious grounds, should rather have been addressed to Leonard. Tolerant though he was, Leonard did not really approve of these

Dame Ethel Smyth, composer, with Virginia Woolf: 'An old woman of seventy-one has fallen in love with me. It's like being caught by a giant crab.'

ardours of Virginia's female admirers, for he thought they disturbed her delicate equilibrium; and Ethel Smyth may well have become aware of this.

By this time, Virginia had had a pavilion or work-room constructed in the garden of Monk's House, with windows that looked out on the water-meadows and the Downs. Here she could be even more isolated for writing than in her room in the house itself. The régime at Monk's House was austere. Both she and Leonard worked there most of the day, and as Leonard has written, even when Virginia took a walk in the afternoons, she was thinking of her next scene, or turning over phrases which she had written in the morning, before she typed them in the later afternoon. It was a life of total dedication. There seems little doubt that it was this life of absorption in her work that Virginia found her deepest satisfaction in; for her, writing, in spite of all the immensely hard work she put into it, was, for most of the time, happiness. At the same time, these periods of undisturbed writing were often interrupted by bouts of intense social activity, which often caused Leonard much anxiety because of the excitement they were apt to cause Virginia. Visiting friends in shoals arrived at Tavistock Square and Monk's House when allowed; and in addition she accepted, when in London, invitations not only to luncheons and dinners with her intimates, but also to grander parties and social occasions where she was one of the chief centres of attraction.

Rosamond and John Lehmann, and
Lytton Strachey, *c.* 1930

For some years, the Woolfs had seen Lytton Strachey only rarely,
though when they did meet relations were as cordial and delightful as
ever. In the late autumn of 1931 Lytton, whose health had been bad
for some time, grew suddenly worse. Virginia had not particularly
liked *Elizabeth and Essex* but admired *Portraits in Miniature* which
followed it. She sent him a copy of *The Waves*, but it is doubtful
whether he ever read it – or was allowed to do more than look at it.
His gradual weakening, his drift towards death, appalled them. On
Christmas Eve, facing the inevitable at last, they wept together at
Monk's House. The news from Ham Spray, Lytton's country home,
however, fluctuated: one day he was better, one day worse. In the
middle of January they drove down, but were not allowed to see him.
A week later he was dead, the first of the 'old Bloomsbury' group of
friends to go. The best doctors had been called in, and had diagnosed
ulcerative colitis: but in fact, after his death, his stomach was found to
be riddled with cancer.

Seven weeks later, Leonard and Virginia, anxious both to see
Ham Spray once more and to try in some measure to console Carrington, went down again. Dora Carrington, who, by her own wish, was
always called Carrington *tout court*, had been an art student when in
1915 she met Lytton. She fell in love, and devoted the rest of her life
to him, though she had many affairs with other younger men (and
women) and in 1921 had married a friend of her brother Noel, Ralph
Partridge, with whom Lytton had fallen in love. On this occasion
Carrington received them, calmly at first, but when alone with
Virginia, broke down. The next morning she shot herself.

Corner of the Studio at Charleston;
painting by Duncan Grant of
Stephen Tomlin's bust of Virginia
Woolf and a painting by Vanessa
Bell in the background, *c.* 1950

Lead cast of Virginia Woolf
by Stephen Tomlin, 1931

Virginia Woolf at Monk's House,
Rodmell, photographed by Leonard
Woolf, *c.* 1937

Leonard Woolf at Rodmell, *c.* 1932

(*Right*) Julian Bell and John Lehmann, *c.* 1930

(*Below*) Julian Bell, photographed by John Lehmann, *c.* 1930

(*Opposite*) Wystan H. Auden at Oxford, photographed by Stephen Spender, *c.* 1927

(*Opposite above right*) Stephen Spender in Hamburg, in a photograph taken by himself, *c.* 1930

(*Opposite below*) Cecil Day Lewis, photographed by Stephen Spender

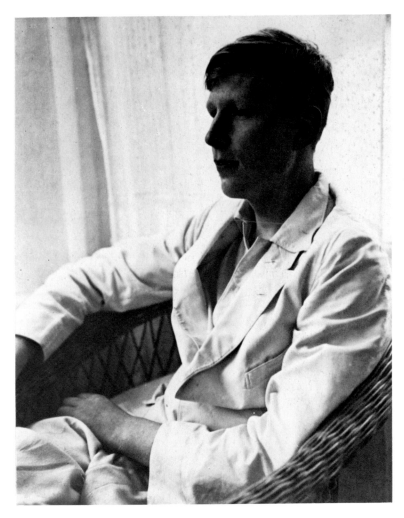

During this period, through Virginia's nephew Julian Bell and his friend, John Lehmann, the latest manager of the Hogarth Press, the Woolfs had begun to see and hear something of a new generation of writers: the young poets who came to be known as the 'Pylon poets', and their friends, the novelists Christopher Isherwood and Edward Upward. Early in 1932, with Michael Roberts as editor, they pub-lished an anthology of the poets, which included W. H. Auden, Stephen Spender and Cecil Day Lewis (who had already appeared in the Hogarth Living Poets series) together with some of the poets of the same generation who had been brought together in two previous anthologies of Cambridge poetry in 1929 and 1930. This book, *New Signatures*, created a certain stir. But Virginia had reservations about the new poets, which she aired in her *Letter to a Young Poet*, also published in 1932. It was meant as an attack (of the most urbane

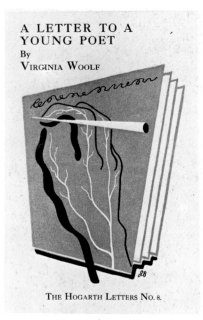

A LETTER TO A YOUNG POET
By
VIRGINIA WOOLF

THE HOGARTH LETTERS NO. 8.

Letter to a Young Poet; the general cover for the Hogarth Letters series, designed by John Banting

sort), but the quotations (as she later admitted herself) were badly chosen to illustrate her argument, and she gave the extraordinary advice to poets not to publish until they were thirty. All right, perhaps, for a novelist; she herself was past thirty when she published her first novel; but if the rule had been observed by, for instance, Shelley and Keats, none of their poetry would exist at all. The lack of sympathy was disappointing; more impressive were some of the incidental remarks. 'Think of yourself', she wrote, criticizing the habit of poets to divide themselves into schools and leaders, 'as something much humbler and less spectacular, but to my mind far more interesting – a poet in whom live all the poets of the past, from whom all poets in time to come will spring . . . you are an immensely ancient, complex, and continuous character, for which reason please treat yourself with respect. . . .'

Scarcely had she finished *The Waves*, when she was off again on one of her 'holiday' books, this time a biography of Elizabeth Barrett Browning's spaniel, Flush. The more she thought about it, the happier she became; in fact she could not talk about it without being con-vulsed with laughter. It was intended as a booklet for Christmas, but in the end it grew into a small book, published in the autumn of 1933, with attractive end-papers designed by Vanessa. The frontispiece was a photograph of their own spaniel, Pinker. It is strange to think that this *jeu d'esprit*, a dog's-eye view of the famous affair between Elizabeth Barrett and Robert Browning, so airy, so sparkling, so

Front end-paper designed by Vanessa Bell for Virginia Woolf's *Flush*: Miss Mitford brings Flush to Elizabeth Barrett

much less fantastical than *Orlando* and so much more warmed by gentle feeling, caused her, after her 'first, fine careless rapture', weeks of gloom, irritation and struggle. But so it was, though no sign of such stress is evident in the text. What is evident, however, is the care with which the Whitechapel chapter has been prepared. She records having rewritten it several times, and read what contemporary accounts she could find of the infamous 'rookeries' that existed in St Giles and other parts of London in the 1840s. It is difficult to escape the inference that she was becoming increasingly aware of, and oppressed by, the dark side of life, that 'sneer behind our backs' of which Neville speaks in *The Waves* when he hears of Percival's death. This awareness was to become insistent in her next novel.

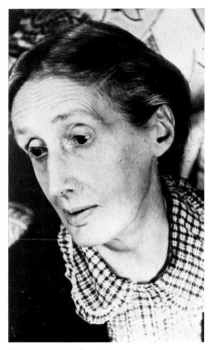

Virginia Woolf, *c.* 1935

It appears to have been while she was writing *Flush,* and also preparing the second volume of her essays, *The Common Reader* (the first volume was published in 1925), that she began to sketch out *The Years.* She saw it, in embryo, as a novel of 'fact', and found herself stored with facts that were ready to pour out the moment she released them by starting work. She had, she claimed, not tried to write such a novel since *Night and Day.* At the beginning of November 1932, she wrote in her diary: 'It's to be an Essay-Novel, called *The Pargiters* – and it's to take in everything, sex, education, life, etc.: and come, with the most powerful and agile leaps, like a chamois, across precipices from 1880 to here and now. That's the notion anyhow, and I have been in such a haze and dream and intoxication, declaiming phrases, seeing scenes as I walk up Southampton Row that I can hardly say I have been alive at all since 10th October.'

What nobody, not even Leonard, seems to have realized is that when she called it an 'Essay-Novel' she meant exactly what she said. It was Professor Mitchell Leaska, of New York University, who first examined the original draft of Chapter I in the Berg Collection of the New York Public Library, and discovered that it in fact consisted of six essays – that is, historical-sociological studies – interspersed with fictional illustrations. Three months later, she was in the process of abolishing these essays, what she now called 'interchapters', and 'compacting them into the text'. But one cannot help thinking that this extraordinary false start, which in conception she obviously thought a great discovery, was the cause of the trouble that followed. It attempted to embrace too much; it ran out of control; it defied a proper artistic resolution. It took her four years to write, and recast again and again; and brought her nearer to the verge of madness than she had been since 1913. The agonies of uncertainty, retyping, rewriting and cutting can be painfully followed in her diary. In the spring of 1936 Leonard had to insist on her breaking off, and drove her down to Cornwall, in the hope that the scenes of her childhood which she loved so much would help to restore her. She came back

feeling much better, but when she started work again at Rodmell the dire symptoms appeared again. She rested for three and a half months, and then she and Leonard agreed that he should read the specially ordered proofs and give his opinion at this stage (which he had previously never done before the final version). Knowing how dangerous the situation was, he praised it rather more than strict truth would have demanded, but told her it was far too long. Relieved, she immediately set to work on a final and ruthless revision and cut out two huge chunks, at least sixteen thousand words. No greater proof of her indomitable courage and of her faith in Leonard's sympathetic judgment could be given. After her death, Leonard expressed the view already mentioned, that, with *Night and Day* and *Three Guineas*, it was one of her three 'dead' books, that is, books in which her visionary power was almost totally absent. Ironically, it was an immediate success on both sides of the Atlantic, and in America it became a best-seller.

Since then, its popularity has dropped sharply, while that of *Mrs Dalloway*, *To the Lighthouse* and *The Waves* has steadily increased. As Leonard observed, the good has driven out the bad. But this long family chronicle, conceived at a time when such family sagas were coming into vogue, starting in 1880, and coming down by unequal stages to the 'present day' (say 1935) has its moments of poetic beauty: for instance, in the section devoted to 1911, where the characters sit 'in a semicircle looking across the meadows at the fading hills' in a moment of peace between generations, and Eleanor, retiring to her room for the night, can only hear 'the heavy laden branches moving up and down in the garden; a cow lowing; a bird chirping, and then, to her delight, the liquid call of an owl going from tree to tree looping them with silver.' Nevertheless, it is a book where evil, squalor, the cruelty of society, are emphasized as never before in Virginia Woolf's work, a world where Antigone – the normal development of womanhood – is 'enclosed, living in a brick tomb ordained by Creon, by male society'. In *A Room of One's Own* Virginia had already shown herself aware of the menace of Mussolini's Fascism; but since then, the hopes of mankind had taken a much steeper plunge, Hitler had risen to power in Germany, the hideous, irrational persecution of the Jews had started, and preparations for war were being made everywhere. One cannot help thinking that Peggy's reflections, in the party that closes the book, are Virginia's own: 'How can one be "happy"? she asked herself, in a world bursting with misery. On every placard at every street corner was death; or worse – tyranny; brutality, torture; the fall of civilization; the end of freedom. We here, she thought, are only sheltering under a leaf, which will be destroyed. . . .' Nothing that Virginia Woolf wrote was ever without distinction of style, language; but in *The Years* something in the very soul of the book sags,

(*Opposite*) Leonard and Virginia Woolf at 52 Tavistock Square, 1939

and is inevitably reflected in the technique. 'Odd little gusts of inconsecutive conversations reached her,' old Eleanor thinks at the party; and that could stand as a description of the dialogue throughout.

The book that followed, *Three Guineas*, begun in January 1937, was in a sense a sequel to *A Room of One's Own* but, as Bernard Blackstone has justly observed, it lacks the 'golden good humour' of that book, and must be seen as representing a deepening of the mood of bitterness, anguish, near-despair that fills *The Years*. It is a forcefully argued and thoroughly documented polemic against male privilege, male prejudice, male vanity, and the state to which male domination has brought the world; but without the urbane wit and balance that made *A Room of One's Own* a delight to read. It is strident, and rather repetitive and marred by a kind of awkwardly inappropriate playfulness in the approach. Since *A Room of One's Own*, even since the writing of *The Years*, the world had gone steadily downhill, the Spanish Civil War had broken out – though the death in that war of her much-loved nephew Julian did not occur until she was well into her work – and the menace of general war vastly increased. She had every reason for her anguish; and yet her remedy for the calamitous state of the world, that women should advance to have an equal voice with men in the running of it, seems almost naïve today. History has not corroborated her belief, or hope, that with women at the helm of affairs nations would cease to be warlike. And yet, if we take her ideal vision of a reformed society, and allow men to belong to it as well as women, we can judge it as deeply moving and inspiring. She, who had refused all honours because she believed them to be contaminated by a corrupt society, conceives of a band of the elect, the outsiders, who would abjure such 'baubles and labels', and devote themselves to a cleansing of values:

They would be creative in their activities, not merely critical. By criticizing education, they would help to create a civilized society which protects culture and intellectual liberty. By criticizing religion they would attempt to free the religious spirit from its present servitude, and would help, if need be, to create a new religion based, it might well be, upon the New Testament, but, it might well be, very different from the religion now erected upon that basis.

As we have already seen, Virginia Woolf began her literary career by writing articles and reviews. She kept up this activity during the whole of her life, and during her long association with Sir Bruce Richmond, Editor of *The Times Literary Supplement*, who found her one of the most skilful and reliable contributors in his team, she wrote innumerable reviews for him, both short and long; all were anonymous, which has added to the difficulty of disinterring them since her death. In May 1938 she notes in her diary: 'A letter, grateful, from Bruce Richmond, ending my 30 years connection with him – the

(Opposite) Virginia Woolf at 52 Tavistock Square in 1939

William Hazlitt, by William Bewick, 1822

William Congreve, by Sir Godfrey Kneller, 1709

Lit. Sup. How pleased I used to be when L. called me "You're wanted by the Major Journal!" and I ran down to the telephone to take my almost weekly orders at Hogarth House! I learnt a lot of my craft writing for him: how to compress; how to enliven; and also was made to read with a pen and notebook, seriously.'

In addition to her work for Richmond, she wrote for many other weeklies and monthlies, English and American, and increasingly as her reputation grew. She was indefatigable; and almost all the time enjoyed the work. Mainly she concerned herself with British and American literature, though occasionally glancing aside to write on one of her favourite French or Russian authors, such as Montaigne or Turgenev. This enormous mass of essays can be roughly divided into four different kinds. There were, first of all, the portraits and assessments of individual writers, which could range throughout English literature from Chaucer to her own contemporaries. Then there were the portraits of well-known but non-literary historical figures, such as Beau Brummell, who happened to be the subject of a book she had been sent to review. Who could appear less 'up her street' than Jack Mytton, that untameable English eccentric and sportsman who set himself alight to cure an attack of hiccups and rode a bear round his drawing-room? And yet her portrait of him is a triumph of humour and empathy. Third, there were the pictures of what she liked to call the 'lives of the obscure', in which she could raise up people who had been dead and forgotten for a hundred years or more and make them, in their fleeting appearances in literary history, live before us, make us laugh at them and sympathize with them. Finally, there were the more general articles, which were often important in relation to her own ideals or aims in writing, such as 'Modern Fiction', 'Mr Bennett and Mrs Brown', and 'The Russian Point of View'. It would perhaps be wrong to call them polemical, as *Three Guineas* is; but certainly after reading them one feels one has been led to a better understanding of the mind that produced *To the Lighthouse* and *The Waves*.

In all the essays her style, perfectly compounded of imagination and wit, is always a delight in its freshness, its sureness of touch, its measured but easy flow; her lucid intelligence plays over everything. Her power of visualization, and her skill in getting to the heart of a subject, are exemplified again and again, above all in her studies of single authors; in, for instance, the pieces on Hazlitt and on Congreve. And in 'Donne after Three Centuries', the essence of John Donne as a character and as a writer seems to be quite effortlessly brought out; in addition, one has the brilliant portrait of Lady Ann Clifford (Countess of Bedford) thrown in as a bonus. Nor does she confine her sympathies to the great figures; she has an extraordinary capacity for making an odd character live, for instance Benjamin Robert

Haydon, in his social surroundings and the significant episodes of his career.

Virginia's gift for developing her theme as narrative, and the strong dramatic instinct she displays, make these studies often more like short stories than criticism. The subjects are alive to her as she writes; she can fix them in one's mind by many devices, frequently by seizing on a crucially illuminating remark, or characteristic, or even appurtenance, and emphasizing it; as when her piece on Christina Rossetti is built round the occasion at a party when 'a little woman dressed in black' announced solemnly '"I am Christina Rossetti" and having so said returned to her chair'; or when she builds up by suggestion after suggestion to her conclusion on De Quincey's *Autobiography*: 'Then suddenly the smooth narrative parts asunder, arch opens beyond arch, the vision of something for ever flying, for ever escaping, is revealed, and time stands still'; or in her analysis of *Robinson Crusoe* when she weaves her argument round the image of 'nothing but a large earthenware pot' staring us 'full in the face'. The most obvious, the most carefully and delightfully contrived example is 'Dr Burney's Evening Party'; but for all the fun and drama she gets out of them, these studies are not fiction. The learning behind them is exact, though lightly carried and never pedantic; her subjects are seen in the focus of a sure and balanced critical judgment. She has, of course, her especial favourites, like Sterne; and in her weaker pieces she may perhaps be accused of an occasional touch of whimsy; but, these infrequent aberrations apart, the cumulative effect of the great body of her critical writing is overwhelming. The scholarship she displays is founded on her voracious reading as a young woman in her father's library, and her amazingly retentive memory; but one must also remember that she found time, and felt it her duty, to read or reread all the relevant material she could get hold of when reviewing a serious work.

In addition to the two volumes of the *Common Reader* published during her lifetime, four further volumes of her critical writings (and short stories) were collected and published by Leonard Woolf after her death, though in no chronological order: *The Death of the Moth, The Moment, The Captain's Death Bed* and *Granite and Rainbow*. It is now certain that this does not constitute the sum total; more of her work is being unearthed every year. In one of these posthumously collected articles, 'The Narrow Bridge of Art', written for the *New York Herald Tribune* in August 1927, she comes back to that self-prophetic vision of the 'new novel' which she had adumbrated some years before in 'Modern Fiction':

And it is possible that there will be among the so-called novels one which we shall scarcely know how to christen. It will be written in prose, but in prose which has

John Donne; engraving by W. Marshall

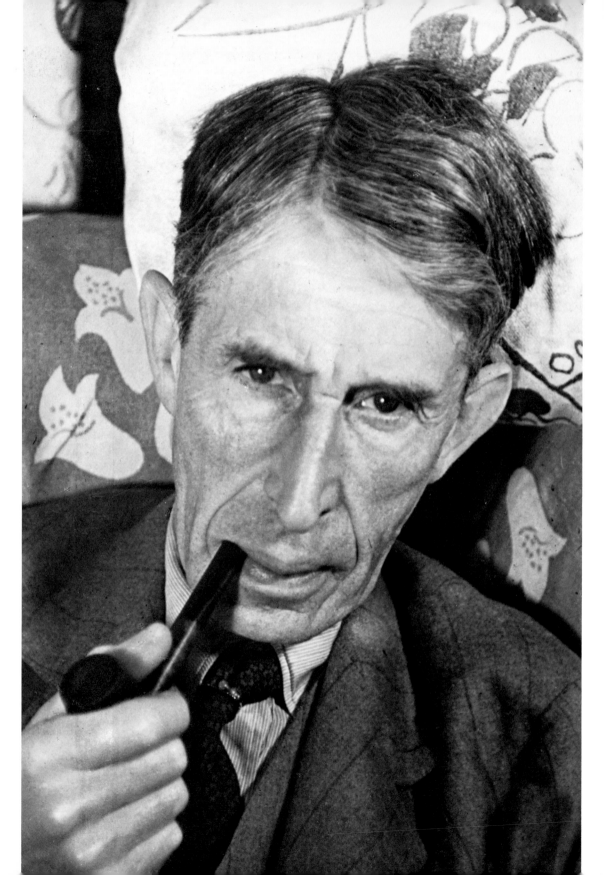

many of the characteristics of poetry. It will have something of the exaltation of poetry, but much of the ordinariness of prose. It will be dramatic, and yet not a play. It will be read, not acted. By what name we are to call it is not a matter of very great importance. . . . It will give the relations of man to nature, to fate; his imagination; his dreams. But it will also give the sneer, the contrast, the question, the closeness and complexity of life. It will take the mould of that queer conglomeration of incongruous things – the modern mind.

It is impossible not to reflect, as one takes one's enchanted way through this miraculous body of critical work, that if Virginia Woolf was known only as a critic, and not also as a novelist, she would count among the greatest of her time. In her study of De Quincey, she writes: 'If we try to analyse our sensations we shall find that we are worked upon as if by music.' Her prose also has something of the charm and spell of music; not of the Romantic era, but of that genius between the formal art of the eighteenth century and the modern, Mozart. At least, so it has seemed to one addicted reader.

In 'The Leaning Tower', a paper read to the Workers' Educational Association at Brighton in May 1940, and her last general essay, Virginia returned to the charge against her younger contemporaries of the *New Signatures* and *New Country* movement, whom she had originally attacked in *Letter to a Young Poet*. Though revealing, in a number of remarkable passages, her sense of the historic importance of the class structure in English literature, and her hope for an eventual transcendence of that structure, it showed once more, regrettably, her lack of sympathy with and comprehension of the ideals that inspired these young writers. Virginia does not seem to have had any deep interest in politics. She was a Socialist basically because Leonard was a Socialist (though not a revolutionary); but Leonard distrusted the extreme left-wing attitudes many of these poets had developed in the years immediately before the war, and something of his distrust had, one suspects, infected her. Nevertheless, the bias she shows in this essay seems all the more extraordinary in view of the fact that in her reading of manuscripts for the Hogarth Press, and in private discussion, she constantly showed an unprejudiced perception of what was promising and creative in this generation. The writers themselves, in particular Louis MacNeice, replied with a cogent defence in *Folios of New Writing* for spring 1941; but by the time the volume was published Virginia herself was dead, and a discussion that might have proved extremely fascinating was cut short.

As soon as she had finished *Three Guineas*, Virginia began to work on her biography of Roger Fry. She had agreed to do this, after his death in 1934, at the insistence of his last love, Helen Anrep, and his sister Margery. Roger had been a very close friend ever since his first appearance in their circle in 1910, and she had delighted in his

(*Opposite*) Leonard Woolf, *c.* 1939

Roger Fry, self-portrait, *c.* 1926

Cassis; painting by Roger Fry

immensely lively mind, the fresh bubble of his ideas in many long discussions they had on painting and the art of writing. After the ill-fated expedition to Constantinople in the spring of 1911 (to study Byzantine art) under his inspiration, and in which he effectively saved Vanessa's life when she fell seriously ill, he had become her sister's lover. At first this caused Virginia considerable dismay, but after the initial period of pique was over, she had been Vanessa's confidante in the affair and Roger was forgiven. After his death, there were moments when she felt that it was an even greater calamity than Lytton's. But one cannot escape the impression that, though she was keen to try her hand at a real biography, a 'solid' book, she regretted her promise before the work was done. She began it in the first week of April 1938, though she had started making notes some years before. Her entries about it in the diary are rarely happy; it is constantly referred to as a 'grind'. 'It's all too minute and tied down – documented,' she records in July, and 'head screwed up over Roger' in October. Worse, when she showed it to Leonard he didn't like it, and gave her 'a very severe lecture'; but Vanessa was deeply moved, and forbade her to alter a word; and Margery Fry was ecstatic. 'It's *him*,' she wrote, and added 'unbounded admiration'.

Roger Fry, a Biography was published at the end of July 1940, and began to boom. A third edition was ordered in less than three weeks; but by then the Battle of Britain had begun, and when London was

Roger Fry in Cambridge, 1932

Self-caricature of Roger Fry, with an omega across his nose referring to the Omega Workshop

bombed the sales of all books slowed down sharply. The reactions of her friends had not all been enthusiastic, nor had the reviews; but Vanessa's and Margery's approval, and the sales success reassured her, and she does not seem to have fallen into one of the usually inevitable pits of depression. When one rereads it today, one cannot fail to admire the skill of the presentation, the way the author effaces herself, the compression of the huge mass of material – letters, articles, books, reminiscences – with which she was faced, and the living portrait of an immensely gifted, wayward, often violently prejudiced, but totally unpompous and deeply serious impresario of painting that emerges; a man who, it has been claimed, radically changed the taste in art of his time and country, and yet was always ready to listen to and reason persuasively with those who disagreed with him. It is in many ways an excellent biography, and here and there one finds quotations that make one feel that Roger Fry's ideas about art entered deeply into Virginia's thoughts about writing. In his introduction to the French section of the catalogue to the second Post-Impressionist Exhibition in 1912, he wrote: 'These artists do not seek to give what can, after all, be but a pale reflex of actual appearance, but to arouse the conviction of a new and definite reality. They do not seek to imitate form, but to create form, not to imitate life, but to find an equivalent for life.'

Nevertheless, it is difficult to see it as an outstandingly important work in the Virginia Woolf canon; rather as a labour of love, flawed by her closeness to the subject and the necessity of concealment of many of the crucial events of the life, but in spite of that carried through with the technical accomplishment she shows in so many of her shorter biographical studies.

One of the reasons why she remained so calm (if one can trust the evidence) about its publication was almost certainly that she was engaged at the same time on a new novel which gave her all but unshadowed delight right up to the penultimate stages, though now and then she records passing headaches following the excitement of writing. At the end of April 1938 comes the first mention: 'But to amuse myself, let me note: Why not *Poyntzet Hall*?' She goes on to suggest its scope, which as so often before differs in many ways from the finished book; but she has already got her basic setting: 'English country; and a scenic old house – and a terrace where nursemaids walk – and people passing – and a perpetual variety and change from intensity to prose. . . .' *Poyntzet Hall* became *Poyntz Hall*; and only at the last moment was rechristened *Between the Acts*.

Opinion has differed greatly about this last novel, which was left without its promised final revision at her death. Many of her admirers have found it altogether too fragmentary and rough, but the present writer agreed, and continues to agree, with what Leonard Woolf wrote to him at the time, directly after her suicide: 'I had expected from what she said and feared to find a loss of vigour. I may be wrong, but it seemed to me the opposite, to be more vigorous and pulled together than most of her other books, to have more depth and to be very moving. I also thought that the strange symbolism gave it an almost terrifying profundity and beauty.' This opinion appears to have gained ground in recent years, and some critics now even consider it her masterpiece, in spite of the fact that the form, as in Michelangelo's last sculptures, has not been completely hewn out of the block of marble. It is, I think, the recognition that she was attempting an entirely new and daring synthesis, and at the same time a microcosmic summing up of the whole of English history, that has led to this shift in opinion.

As I have already pointed out, during the writing of *The Years* and *Three Guineas*, Virginia Woolf had become increasingly conscious of the dark side of life, of the power of evil; as exemplified, above all, by the rise of Hitler and the persecution of the Jews and other minorities in Germany; and by the Civil War in Spain which had already claimed her nephew Julian as a victim. Before she had gone any distance with *Between the Acts*, the surrender at Munich had taken place; though happy, the work was slow because she was still writing *Roger Fry*; and the first draft was still far from complete

(*Opposite*) Page from the final typescript of *Between the Acts*, with Virginia Woolf's manuscript corrections and Leonard Woolf's editorial annotations

a few head with no hair on it. He turned.

"Heel!" he bawled, "Heel , you brute!" And George turned;
and the nurses turned holding the furry bear; they all turned
to look at Sohrab the Aghan hound bounding and bouncing
among the flowers.

"Heel!" the old man bawled, as if he were commanding a
regiment . It was impressive, to the nurses, the way
an old boy of his age could still bawl and make a brute like
that obey him. Back came the Aghan hound, sidling, apologetic
And as he cringed at the old man's feet, a string was slipped
over his collar; the noose that old Oliver always carried
with him.

"You wild beast...you bad beast" he grumbled, stooping.
George looked at the dog only. The hairy flanks were sucked
in and out; there was a blob of foam on its nostrils. He burst
out crying.

Old Oliver raised himself, his veins swollen, his cheeks
flushed; he was angry. His little game with the paper hadn't
worked. The boy was a cry-baby. He nodded and sauntered on,
smoothing out the crumpled paper and muttering, as he tried
to find his line in the column, "A cry-baby--a cry-baby".
But the breeze blew the great sheet out; and over the edge
he surveyed the landscape-- flowing fields, heath and woods;
Framed, they became a picture. Had he been a painter, he would
have fixed his easel here, where the country, barred by
trees, looked like a picture. Then the breeze fell.

"M. Daladier" he read finding his place in the column,
"has been successful in pegging down the franc...."

Leave 2 lines white ⟶

when war broke out. In the novel she attempts to incorporate her new vision of the dialectic of history, and of the existence of an obverse everywhere to the coin of beauty. Its basic underlying themes are the struggle of civilization against savagery; of what is spiritually inspiring against squalor and greed; of love against lust, against what is destructive and selfish in sexual appetite.

The action, as in *Mrs Dalloway*, takes place in a single day and a single place: the day of the annual village pageant at Pointz Hall. But there is a brief prelude, the evening before; and in that prelude all the main themes are, almost imperceptibly, stated. In the opening three or four paragraphs one has the first contrast: it is a beautiful summer's night, but they are talking about a cesspool: 'What a subject to talk about on a night like this!' exclaims one of the guests. She thinks she hears a nightingale, but is told that it is 'a daylight bird, chuckling over the substance and succulence of the day, over worms, snails, grit'. Immediately the immense antiquity of the country is emphasized, as it is re-emphasized again and again in the course of the book. The rise of one phase of civilization in the history of England is hinted at, and in its destruction the rise of another: the site chosen for the cesspool is on the Roman road, and from an aeroplane one can still see, plainly marked, 'the scars made by the Britons; by the Romans; by the Elizabethan manor house; and by the plough, when they ploughed the hill to grow wheat in the Napoleonic Wars'. A few lines later Isa, the daughter-in-law of old Mr Oliver who owns the house, comes in and sees Rupert Haines, the neighbouring gentleman farmer after whom she lusts. Mr Oliver quotes Byron's love-lyrics, and Isa sees the words 'like two rings, perfect rings, that floated them, herself and Haines, like two swans down stream. But his snow-white breast was circled with a tangle of dirty duckweed, and she too, in her webbed feet was entangled, by her husband, the stockbroker.'

So the stage is set for the narrative proper, in which these themes are developed and repeated. Mr Oliver's old sister, Mrs Swithin, is reading an 'Outline of History', and dreams of 'rhododendron forests in Piccadilly'. The great barn in which the refreshments are served 'had been built over seven hundred years ago and reminded some people of a Greek Temple, others of the middle ages, most people of an age before their own'. As Isa lusts after Rupert Haines, so her husband Giles lusts after Mrs Manresa, one of the guests, a vulgarian and extrovert, who thinks of herself as 'a wild child of nature', and appears mysteriously accompanied by William Dodge, artist and invert. William finds unspoken understanding from Isa, arouses the hatred of Giles, and feels a spiritual peace in the presence of Mrs Swithin, who is religious and 'one of the unifiers' while her brother, Mr Oliver, is a rationalist, a 'separatist'. Into this scene of civilized behaviour and outward order, Virginia Woolf injects the violent report of the

Angelica at the Piano; painting by
Duncan Grant, 1940

guardsmen who lured a girl into their barracks with their talk of 'a
horse with a green tail' and raped her there (a true story), and the
violent happenings on the other side of the Channel, where innocent
men are being murdered, which haunt Giles and make him feel
disgusted with the pageant and the so complacent-seeming people
around him. War threatens, he thinks continually; Bolney Minster
and all the peaceful scene can be smashed to pieces; and as if to
underline his thoughts a flight of aeroplanes roars overhead as the
Vicar is addressing the audience at the end.

It is impossible in a short space to examine all the thematic strands
intertwined in the rainbow texture of the book, or to call attention
to all the scintillating images, filled with what Leonard had called
'an almost terrifying profundity and beauty'. One brief episode
remains in mind as being of particular symbolic significance, when
Isa's little boy experiences a true 'moment of being' as he grubs in

the grass at the root of one of the ancient trees in the garden: 'The flower blazed between the angles of the roots. Membrane after membrane was torn. It blazed a soft yellow, a lambent light under a film of velvet; it filled the caverns behind the eyes with light. All that inner darkness became a hall, leaf smelling, earth smelling of yellow light. And the tree was beyond the flower; the grass, the flower and the tree were entire.' But even as the child experiences this eternal moment, 'there was a roar and a hot breath and a stream of coarse grey hair rushed between him and the flower' – his grandfather is playing a cruel joke on him, appearing as 'a terrible peaked eyeless monster', imaging the destructive horror of the world.

During the pageant the words of the actors, and of the song repeatedly sung by the villagers weaving in and out of the trees throughout the production, and so representing the continuity of anonymous life, are blown away by the wind again and again. They come to the audience only in fragments, as they themselves are only 'orts, scraps and fragments'; and as one approaches the conclusion of the book it is difficult to escape the impression that Virginia Woolf's underlying message is coming to one in fragmentary but brilliant stabs of poetic illumination, as it were the incoherent-seeming, vatic cries of an ancient oracle, that need to be pondered with all the powers of one's imagination to reveal their meaning.

At the end, Miss La Trobe, the strange, uncouth, solitary author and producer of the pageant, surely image of the prophetic artist Virginia now felt herself to be, is left with the feeling that she has once more failed to communicate, and yet with a triumph; but 'it was in the giving that the triumph was'. She goes to the village pub, and there she has a new vision: '"I should group them", she murmured, "here." It would be midnight; there would be two figures, half concealed by a rock. The curtain would rise. What would the first words be? The words escaped her.'

Miss La Trobe's vision becomes in fact the coda of the book. Giles and Isa are left alone, in a night 'that dwellers in caves had watched from some high place among the rocks'. In this emblematic aloneness, 'enmity was bared; also love. Before they slept, they must fight; after they had fought, they would embrace. From that embrace another life might be born. But first they must fight, as the dog fox fights with the vixen, in the heart of darkness, in the fields of night.'

It is astonishing to think that, even when she was on the last lap of this challenging adventure, Virginia Woolf already envisaged a book to follow it, perhaps a kind of history of English literature, to be called *Anon*. Notes, and even a few chapters in draft, exist for this book, but it was never to be written. What the sheer existence of the project shows is that the fountain of her creative energy had in no way been dried up by the ominous progress of the war and the reverses

in Britain's fortunes that 1940 brought with it. She was fully aware of the danger in which the country stood after the defeat of France, and at the back of her mind loomed the suicide pact she had made with Leonard in the event of invasion. But when the fighting began in the air over southern England, and the possibility of successful national resistance was entertained again, in some way she was rather exhilarated than frightened, as people who suffer from inward terrors of the mind can often be relieved by the crystallization of outward terrors. Even the bombing of London and the setting on fire of their new house in Mecklenburgh Square, whither they had also moved the Hogarth Press, followed by the destruction of their old house in Tavistock Square, did not check her mood that seemed almost like euphoria. Her friends reported that she was in good spirits, happy particularly in her simplified country life, free from the necessity of

Mecklenburgh Square in 1937; No. 37 has 'Flat to Let' sign

37
Mecklenburgh Square,
W.C.1.

Terminus 7585.
29th July

Dear John,

I handed on your message to Leonard, & we're both very sorry you couldn't come to Monks House, & that your mother's ill again: Please give her my sympathy. We could have offered you a great variety of air raid alarms, distant bombs, reports by Mrs Bleach who brought a stirrup pump (installed, neither today in my bedroom) of battles out at sea. Indeed its rather lovely about 2 in the morning to see the lights stalking the Germans over the marsh. But this remains on tap, & you must propose yourself later. And let me know if you want to meet the Major & hear about — what was it? — Why the Crab walks sideways!

Leonard's tackling Mrs N. downstairs — showers of confidences & complaints, also

(*Opposite*) Letter by Virginia Woolf to John Lehmann, 29 July 1940

Posthumous re-issue of *Monday or Tuesday* with a number of further stories, prepared by Leonard Woolf for publication as decided by Virginia Woolf before her death. The jacket design is by Vanessa Bell

breasting her formal social round in London. To a younger friend who was unable to accept an invitation to visit Rodmell, she wrote: 'We could have offered you a great variety of air-raid alarms, distant bombs, reports by Mrs Bleach who brought a stirrup pump (installed, needless to say, in my bedroom), of battles out at sea. Indeed it's rather lovely about 2 in the morning to see the lights stalking the Germans over the marshes. But this remains on tap, so you must propose yourself later.'

Replica of Stephen Tomlin's lead cast of Virginia Woolf, in the garden of Monk's House, Rodmell

Unfortunately, this mood did not survive the trauma of finishing *Between the Acts*. We know that she wrote several versions (which still exist), but by the time she had completed the version which she showed to Leonard late in February 1941, she had lost faith in it. At the end of January 1941, Leonard had been sufficiently alarmed about her mental state to persuade her to see Octavia Wilberforce, a remark-able woman who had more or less become her doctor, and lived close by in Brighton. Virginia got better, but the improvement did not last. It was *The Waves* and *The Years* all over again. 'The fact is,' she wrote, 'it was written in the intervals of doing *Roger* with my brain half asleep. I didn't realise how bad it was till I read it over.' She said she would revise it once more; but even as she wrote, she felt the symptoms of madness rising in her mind again. This time she was convinced that the terrifying voices could not be held at bay, and the praise and enthusiasm of Leonard and myself were unavailing. She carried out the plan that had long been in her mind for such a crisis, wrote farewell letters to Leonard and Vanessa, filled her pockets with stones and went out and drowned herself in the River Ouse. Her body was not recovered for three weeks.

(*Opposite*) Leonard Woolf reading Virginia Woolf's diary, *c*. 1960

In the garden of Monk's House there were two tall elms with branches interlacing, which the Woolfs had liked to call Leonard and Virginia. After her cremation, Virginia's ashes were buried at the base of one of these elms, which blew down in a great gale two years later. The other elm is still standing. Since Leonard's death, the replica of the National Portrait Gallery's bust of Virginia by Stephen Tomlin and the memorial plaque below it have been moved to one of the little low flint walls that divide up the garden, and a bust of Leonard, also with a plaque, has been put up at the other end of the wall. Both face away from the house, towards Virginia's garden work-room.

Needlework design for a chair cover by Vanessa Bell, worked by Virginia Woolf

ACKNOWLEDGMENTS

BIBLIOGRAPHY

CHRONOLOGY

LIST OF ILLUSTRATIONS

INDEX

ACKNOWLEDGMENTS

Anyone who writes on Virginia Woolf today cannot fail to be deeply in debt to Professor Quentin Bell's massively detailed two-volume biography of his aunt, and to the five volumes of Leonard Woolf's autobiography. I express my grateful thanks to the former and to his sister Angelica (Mrs David Garnett) for permission to quote extensively from Virginia Woolf's works and letters, to Mrs Ian Parsons for permission to quote from the latter, and in both cases to the publishers, The Hogarth Press. Acknowledgments are also due to Professor Bell and Messrs Chatto and Windus for a quotation from Clive Bell's *Old Friends*, and to Mr David Garnett and the same publishers for a quotation from *The Flowers of the Forest*; to Miss Rosamond Lehmann for permission to quote from her essay on Virginia Woolf which originally appeared in *Penguin New Writing* and subsequently in Joan Russell Noble's compilation *Recollections of Virginia Woolf*; and to Mr Nigel Nicolson for a quotation from a letter of his mother to Virginia Woolf. I must finally thank Professor Mitchell Leaska of New York University for allowing me to refer to his remarkable discovery about the origin of *The Years*, which is described in his edition of *The Pargiters*, the original draft of the novel (1978).

BIBLIOGRAPHY

The standard edition of Virginia Woolf's work is the Uniform Edition published in seventeen volumes (1929–55) by The Hogarth Press, London, and Harcourt Brace Jovanovich, Inc., New York. It includes *A Room of One's Own* and *Three Guineas*, which, like the novels, are widely available in paperback editions. Virginia Woolf's biography of Roger Fry (1940) was reprinted in 1979. Her short stories, collected in various volumes during her lifetime and after her death, have been reissued in a single volume by The Hogarth Press (1985).

Her essays, including the two volumes of *The Common Reader* and many uncollected in her lifetime, were arranged by Leonard Woolf in four volumes, *Collected Essays* (1966–7). They are now being reissued in a new multi-volume edition by Andrew McNeillie (1986–). There is a useful selection of the literary and biographical writings in *Books and Portraits*, edited by Mary Lyon (1977). Virginia Woolf's letters have been published in six volumes (1975–80), edited by Nigel Nicolson and Joanne Trautmann; her diaries, edited by Anne Olivier Bell, are published in five volumes (1977–84). *Women and Writing* (1979) is a collection of Virginia Woolf's writings on women and feminism. The play *Freshwater*, mentioned on page 71, was published in 1976, in an edition by Lucio P. Ruotolo.

Virginia Woolf's autobiographical writings are collected in *Moments of Being* (2nd ed., 1985). Quentin Bell's authoritative *Virginia Woolf: A Biography* (1972) remains the standard biography, but is usefully complemented in some respects by Lyndall Gordon's *Virginia Woolf: A Writer's Life* (1984). Leonard Woolf's autobiography was published in five volumes 1960–9 and reissued in two volumes by Oxford University Press in 1980. There is a biography of Leonard Woolf by Duncan Wilson (1978).

Quentin Bell's *Bloomsbury* (1968) is the best single-volume survey of Virginia Woolf's milieu. Noël Annan's *Leslie Stephen* (2nd ed., 1984) gives a detailed picture of her family background. Important memoirs include Clive Bell's *Old Friends* (1956) and volume two of David Garnett's reminiscences, *Flowers of the Forest* (1955). See also *Recollections of Virginia Woolf*, edited by John Russell Noble (1972), which has twenty-seven contributions. Biographies which throw light on Virginia Woolf include *Vanessa Bell* by Frances Spalding (1983), *Lytton Strachey* by Michael Holroyd (2 vols., 1967 and 1968) and *Vita Sackville-West* by Victoria Glendinning (1983). Vita Sackville-West's letters to Virginia Woolf, edited by Louise DeSalvo and Mitchell A. Leaska, were published in 1984. *Deceived with Kindness* (1984) by Vanessa Bell's daughter, Angelica Garnett, is a remarkable account of a Bloomsbury childhood and its effects.

B. J. Kirkpatrick's *A Bibliography of Virginia Woolf* (3rd ed., 1980) and *Virginia Woolf: The Critical Heritage*, a collection of contemporary reviews edited by Robin Majumdar and Allen McLaurin (1975), are basic sources. Further reading might include E. M. Forster's Rede Lecture *Virginia Woolf*, reprinted in his *Two Cheers for Democracy* (1951), and Erich Auerbach's chapter on *To the Lighthouse* in his *Mimesis* (1953), a classic critical discussion. J. W. Graham's edition of the two holograph drafts of *The Waves* (1976) gives an unparalleled opportunity to study Virginia Woolf at work.

CHRONOLOGY

1882 25 January: Birth of Virginia Stephen, third child of Leslie Stephen and Julia Duckworth (née Jackson) at 22 Hyde Park Gate, Kensington. Sister Vanessa born 1879, brothers Thoby 1880 and Adrian 1883.

1895 May: Death of Mrs Leslie Stephen. Virginia has first breakdown that summer.

1897 July: Stella Duckworth, Virginia's half-sister, dies.

1899 September: Thoby enters Trinity College, Cambridge, at same time as Lytton Strachey, Leonard Woolf, Clive Bell and Saxon Sydney-Turner.

1904 22 February: Death of (Sir) Leslie Stephen. 10 May: Beginning of Virginia's second serious breakdown. 14 December: Virginia's first publication, unsigned review in the *Guardian*.

1905 Thoby Stephen starts 'Thursday Evenings' at 46 Gordon Square, to which address all Stephen children have moved.

1906 September: Stephen children make expedition to Greece, Violet Dickinson with them. 20 November: Thoby dies in London of typhoid fever contracted in Greece. 22 November: Vanessa agrees to marry Clive Bell.

1907 April: Virginia and Adrian leave Gordon Square and take up residence at 29 Fitzroy Square. They renew 'Thursday Evenings' at new address.

1908 February: Julian Bell born to Vanessa and Clive.

1909 February: Lytton Strachey proposes marriage to Virginia; is accepted, but engagement cancelled shortly after.

1910 10 February: 'The Dreadnought hoax'. August: Birth of Claudian, later re-named Quentin, Bell. November: Opening of first Post-Impressionist Exhibition, arranged by Roger Fry at Grafton Galleries.

1911 July: Leonard Woolf, on leave from Ceylon, dines at 46 Gordon Square and meets Virginia again. August: Virginia stays at The Old Vicarage, Grantchester, with Rupert Brooke. November: Virginia starts living at 38 Brunswick Square, W.C.1, with Adrian, Maynard Keynes, Duncan Grant and (in December) Leonard Woolf. Virginia takes Asheham House, Sussex.

1912 May: Leonard resigns from Colonial Service and Virginia agrees to marry him. They are married in August and spend honeymoon on Continent.

1913 April: *The Voyage Out* (originally called *Melymbrosia*) accepted for publication by Duckworth. In summer Virginia begins to be seriously ill, and in September attempts suicide.

1914 February: Virginia apparently cured of mental illness.

1915 L. and V. take Hogarth House, Richmond. By end of February Virginia begins to be seriously ill again. March: *The Voyage Out* published. November: Virginia once more on road to recovery.

1917 L. and V. order a hand printing machine and start Hogarth Press.

1918 May: Publication of Lytton Strachey's *Eminent Victorians*.

1919 May: *Night and Day* accepted by Duckworth and published in October. Hogarth Press publishes *Kew Gardens* and T.S. Eliot's *Poems*. July: L. and V. buy Monk's House, Rodmell, having left Asheham.

1921 March: *Monday or Tuesday* published.

1922 October: *Jacob's Room* published. December: Virginia meets Vita Sackville-West (Mrs Harold Nicolson) at dinner party given by Clive Bell.

1924 January: Virginia buys lease of 52 Tavistock Square, to which they move in March, with Hogarth Press. July: George Rylands becomes trainee manager at Hogarth Press. November–December: George Rylands leaves Hogarth Press, and is succeeded as trainee manager by Angus Davidson.

1925 April: *The Common Reader* published. May: *Mrs Dalloway* published.

1927 May: *To the Lighthouse* published. October: Virginia starts to write *Orlando*. December: Angus Davidson leaves Hogarth Press.

1928 April–June: Virginia awarded *Femina Vie Heureuse* prize. October: *Orlando* published, and Virginia spends week in France with Vita. Virginia visits Cambridge and reads at Girton and Newnham Colleges two papers which form basis of *A Room of One's Own*.

1929 October: *A Room of One's Own* published.

1930 February: Virginia first meets Ethel Smyth, who becomes constant visitor.

1931 January: John Lehmann begins as trainee manager at Hogarth Press. April: L. and V. make tour of France by car, and visit Montaigne's Tower. October: *The Waves* published. Before and after publication Virginia suffers from severe headaches and depression.

1932 January: Death of Lytton Strachey. April–May: L. and V. make tour of Greece with Roger and Margery Fry. July: *Letter to a Young Poet* published. September: John Lehmann leaves Hogarth Press. October: *The Common Reader* (Second Series) published.

1933 October: *Flush* published.

1934 September: Death of Roger Fry.

1935 January: Virginia's play *Freshwater* performed by family and friends in Vanessa's studio at 8 Fitzroy Square. All this year and next Virginia writing and rewriting *The Years* under great mental strain.

1937 March: *The Years* published. Julian Bell returns from China and joins International Brigade in Spanish Civil War; in July is killed.

1938 John Lehmann returns to Hogarth Press, and in March takes over Virginia's half-share in Hogarth Press. June: *Three Guineas* published.

1939 August: L. and V. move from 52 Tavistock Square to 37 Mecklenburgh Square, and take Hogarth Press with them.

1940 April: Virginia gives lecture (*The Leaning Tower*) to Workers' Educational Association in Brighton. July: *Roger Fry, a Biography* published. September: 37 Mecklenburgh Square badly damaged by fire bombs. Hogarth Press moved to Garden City Press at Letchworth.

1941 February: Virginia finishes *Between the Acts*. March: Virginia's mental health deteriorating again. On 28 March she drowns herself in the River Ouse.

LIST OF ILLUSTRATIONS

Lytton Strachey and Clive Bell criticizing works of art; pen and ink drawing by Henry Lamb.

26 Virginia Woolf and Lytton Strachey ice-skating; sketch by Dora Carrington, from a letter to Lytton Strachey, 4 February 1917, published in *Letters and Extracts from her Diaries*, London 1970.

27 The Dreadnought hoax; front page of *The Daily Mirror*, 16 February 1910.

28 Duncan Grant, 1911; pencil drawing by Henry Lamb.

Duncan Grant, Maynard Keynes and Clive Bell at Charleston. *By permission of Professor Quentin Bell.*

29 Adrian Stephen and his wife Karin (née Costelloe), *c.* 1914. *By permission of Mrs Angelica Garnett.*

30 Vanessa Bell, *Asheham House*, 1912. Oil on board, $18\frac{7}{8} \times 21\frac{1}{8}$ ins. Private collection.

'Asheham as you perceive is surrounded by sunshine. . . .' Sketch by Dora Carrington, from a letter to Lytton Strachey of 29 January 1917, published in *Letters and Extracts from her Diaries*, London 1970.

31 Duncan Grant, *Asheham Group*, 1913 (Henri Doucet, Virginia Woolf, Vanessa Bell and Adrian Stephen). Oil on board, 10×25 ins. *Anthony d'Offay Gallery, London.*

Leonard and Virginia Woolf at Asheham House. *By permission of Mrs Angelica Garnett.*

32 Leonard Woolf at work; oil painting by Vanessa Bell, $32 \times 25\frac{1}{2}$ ins. *National Portrait Gallery, London.*

33 Virginia Woolf; pencil and watercolour sketch by Vanessa Bell.

34 Ka Cox, 1912; oil on wooden panel by Duncan Grant, $36\frac{3}{4} \times 20\frac{1}{2}$ ins. *Fry Collection, Courtauld Institute Galleries, London.*

36 Vanessa Bell, *Virginia Woolf Seated*, 1912. Oil on board, $14\frac{1}{2} \times 12$ ins. *Anthony d'Offay Gallery, London. Photo Eileen Tweedy.*

37 Rupert Brooke, 1919; woodcut by Gwen Raverat, published in Brooke's *Collected Poems*, London 1919.

Mark Gertler, *The Pond at Garsington*, 1916. Oil, 25×25 ins. *Leeds Art Galleries.*

37 Lady Ottoline Morrell, *c.* 1912; drawing by Henry Lamb. *National Portrait Gallery, London.*

38 Virginia Woolf and Lytton Strachey at Garsington; photograph by Lady Ottoline Morrell. Private collection.

Lytton Strachey, Clive Bell and Duncan Grant at Eleanor House, Sussex, 1915. *By permission of Mrs Angelica Garnett.*

Duncan Grant and E. M. Forster, standing behind Clive Bell and Mary Hutchinson in the garden at Charleston Farm. *By permission of Mrs Angelica Garnett.*

39 Charleston Farm. *Photo Ann James.*

Duncan Grant's studio at Charleston, *c.* 1930–31.

40 Farringdon Street, Holborn Viaduct, December 1925. *Photo Radio Times Hulton Picture Library.*

41 Advertisement included at the back of the Hogarth Press edition of Gorky's *Reminiscences of Tolstoi*, 1920.

42 T. S. Eliot, 1938; drawing by Wyndham Lewis. *Courtesy of the Harvard University Portrait Collection, given to Eliot House, Harvard University, by Mrs Stanley Resor of New York City.*

Katherine Mansfield. *Photo Radio Times Hulton Picture Library.*

43 The cover of Virginia Woolf's *Kew Gardens*, designed by Vanessa Bell, 1919. *Anthony d'Offay Gallery, London.*

44 Arnold Bennett, *c.* 1926; drawing by B. Partridge. *National Portrait Gallery, London.*

45 H. G. Wells. *Photo Radio Times Hulton Picture Library.*

47 Original drawing by Vanessa Bell for the jacket of *A Writer's Diary*, London 1953. *Anthony d'Offay Gallery, London. Photo Eileen Tweedy.*

49 Monk's House, Rodmell, seen from the road. *Photo Ann James.*

50 Drawing by Vanessa Bell for the jacket of *Mrs Dalloway*, 1925. *Anthony d'Offay Gallery, London. Photo Eileen Tweedy.*

51 Walter Sickert, *The Wonderful Month of May*. Oil on canvas, $22\frac{1}{2} \times 25$ ins. *Courtesy Museum of Fine Arts, Boston.*

52 Virginia Woolf, 1921; pencil and wash sketch by Wyndham Lewis. *Victoria and Albert Museum, London.*

53 Bus traffic on the Strand, August 1923. *Photo London Transport Executive.*

82, Letter about *The Waves* from
83 Virginia Woolf to John Lehmann, 17 September 1931.

84 Duncan Grant, *The Farm Pond near Firle, Sussex*, 1930–32. Oil on canvas, 31$\frac{3}{8}$ × 51$\frac{1}{2}$ ins. *Art Gallery of Ontario, gift of Reuben Wells Leonard Estate, 1932. Photo Brigdens, courtesy Gallery.*

86 Sir Hugh Walpole. *Radio Times Hulton Picture Library.*

87 Dame Ethel Smyth with Virginia Woolf. *By permission of Mrs T. Parsons.*

88 Rosamond and John Lehmann with Lytton Strachey, *c.* 1930.

89 Duncan Grant, *Corner of the Studio at Charleston, c.* 1950 (Stephen Tomlin's bust of Virginia Woolf, with a painting by Vanessa Bell in the background). Oil on board, 30 × 20 ins. *Anthony d'Offay Gallery, London. Photo Eileen Tweedy.*

Virginia Woolf, 1931; lead cast by Stephen Tomlin. *National Portrait Gallery, London.*

90 Virginia Woolf at Rodmell, *c.* 1937, in a photograph by Leonard Woolf. *By permission of Drew Ponder-Greene.*

Virginia Woolf at Rodmell, *c.* 1937, in a photograph by Leonard Woolf. *By permission of Drew Ponder-Greene.*

91 Leonard Woolf at Rodmell, *c.* 1932. *Photo Ramsey and Muspratt, Cambridge.*

92 Julian Bell and John Lehmann, *c.* 1930.

Julian Bell, *c.* 1930; photographed by John Lehmann.

93 Wystan Hugh Auden at Oxford, *c.* 1927; photographed by Stephen Spender.

Stephen Spender in Hamburg, *c.* 1930, in a photograph taken by himself.

Cecil Day Lewis; photographed by Stephen Spender.

94 *Letter to a Young Poet*; the general cover for the Hogarth Letters series, designed by John Banting.

Front end-paper designed by Vanessa Bell for Virginia Woolf's *Flush*: Miss Mitford brings Flush to Elizabeth Barrett. *Photo Eileen Tweedy.*

95 Virginia Woolf, *c.* 1935. *Photo Gisèle Freund.*

96 Leonard and Virginia Woolf at 52 Tavistock Square, 1939. *Photo Gisèle Freund.*

99 Virginia Woolf at 52 Tavistock Square, 1939. *Photo Gisèle Freund.*

100 William Hazlitt, 1822; chalk portrait by William Bewick, 22$\frac{3}{4}$ × 14$\frac{3}{4}$ ins. *National Portrait Gallery, London.*

William Congreve, 1709; oil portrait by Sir Godfrey Kneller, 36 × 28 ins. *National Portrait Gallery, London.*

101 John Donne; engraving by W. Marshall.

102 Leonard Woolf, *c.* 1939. *Photo Gisèle Freund.*

104 Roger Fry, self-portrait, *c.* 1926.

Roger Fry, *Cassis. Musée d'Art Moderne, Paris.*

105 Roger Fry in Cambridge, 1932. *Photo Ramsey and Muspratt, Cambridge.*

Self-caricature of Roger Fry; the omega across his nose refers to the Omega Workshop. *Fry Collection, Courtauld Institute of Art, London.*

107 Page from the final typescript of *Between the Acts*, with Virginia Woolf's manuscript corrections and Leonard Woolf's editorial annotations. *Henry W. and Albert A. Berg Collection, The New York Public Library, Astor, Lenox and Tilden Foundations.*

109 Duncan Grant, *Angelica at the Piano*, 1940. *Tate Gallery, London.*

111 Mecklenburgh Square in 1937. *Photo Greater London Council.*

112 Letter by Virginia Woolf to John Lehmann, 29 July 1940. *Henry W. and Albert A. Berg Collection, The New York Public Library, Astor, Lenox and Tilden Foundations.*

113 Jacket design by Vanessa Bell, *c.* 1943, for *A Haunted House and Other Stories*, the posthumous reissue of *Monday or Tuesday* with a number of further stories. *Anthony d'Offay Gallery, London. Photo Eileen Tweedy.*

114 Replica of Stephen Tomlin's lead cast of Virginia Woolf, in the garden of Monk's House, Rodmell.

115 Leonard Woolf reading Virginia Woolf's diary, *c.* 1960. *Photo Gisèle Freund.*

116 Needlework design for a chair cover by Vanessa Bell, worked by Virginia Woolf.

INDEX